The 12 Step Prayer Book

T0053667

The 12 Step Prayer Book

A Collection of Inspirational Daily Readings

Third edition, compiled

WRITTEN AND COMPILED BY
BILL P. AND LISA D.

Hazelden
Publishing

Hazelden Publishing
Center City, Minnesota
800-328-9000
hazelden.org/bookstore

The 12 Step Prayer Book, third edition, compiled
© 2019 by Hazelden Foundation
The 12 Step Prayer Book, first edition published by Glen Abbey Books
Inc., 1990. First published by Hazelden Foundation, 1999;
second edition published 2004.
The 12 Step Prayer Book Volume 2 published 2007 by Hazelden Foundation.
All rights reserved. Produced in the United States of America.

Library of Congress Cataloging-in-Publication Data

Names: P., Bill, 1947– author. | D., Lisa, author.
Title: The 12 step prayer book : a collection of inspirational daily readings /
   written and compiled by Bill P. and Lisa D.
Other titles: Twelve step prayer book
Description: Third edition, compiled. | Center City : Hazelden Publishing, 2019.
   | Series: Hazelden meditations | Includes index.
Identifiers: LCCN 2019022784 (print) | LCCN 2019022785 (ebook) | ISBN
   9781616498863 (paperback) | ISBN 9781616498870 (ebook)
Subjects: LCSH: Alcoholics—Prayers and devotions. | Devotional calendars.
   | Twelve-step programs—Religious aspects—Christianity—Meditations.
Classification: LCC BV4596.A48 A12 2019 (print) | LCC BV4596.A48 (ebook)
   | DDC 204/.33—dc22
LC record available at https://lccn.loc.gov/2019022784
LC ebook record available at https://lccn.loc.gov/2019022785

24 23 22   3 4 5 6

INTERIOR DESIGN BY TERRI KINNE
TYPESETTING BY PERCOLATOR

Editor's notes

The 12 Step Prayer Book and *The 12 Step Prayer Book Volume 2* have been combined into one comprehensive book. Every effort was made to determine the source of each prayer and reading included in this new edition, as explained in the book's introduction. Each reading's source information appears in the List of Readings and Attributions near the end of the book.

The Twelve Steps come from *Alcoholics Anonymous*, 4th ed., (New York: Alcoholics Anonymous World Services, 2001). These sources all come from Hazelden Publishing: *The Language of Letting Go* by Melody Beattie, 1990; *A Day at a Time: Daily Reflections for Recovering People*, 1989; *The Little Red Book*, rev. ed., 1986; *Twenty-Four Hours a Day*, rev. ed., 1975; *Touchstones: A Book of Daily Meditations for Men*, 2nd ed., 1991.

This publication is intended to support personal growth and should not be thought of as a substitute for the advice of health care professionals. The authors' advice and viewpoints are their own.

In the process of being reissued in 2019, *The 12 Step Prayer Book* has undergone minor editing updates and been retypeset in the Whitman font family.

*This book is dedicated
to the memory of
Patrick and Aimee Mott Butler
St. Paul, Minnesota
and to
Margaret R. Graves*

Contents

Introduction

A Roadmap for Reading and Recovery

A lifetime consists of roughly 30,000 days, each one a chapter. Each will have its beginning, its dips and swells, and its end. Tomorrow you will turn another page and tell another story. You must figure out which are your favorite endings for each chapter, and write the day with them. Use these prayers to inspire your daily tales of strength, grace, and hope.

These 366 prayers and readings were originally published as two different volumes: *The 12 Step Prayer Book* in 1990 and *The 12 Step Prayer Book Volume 2* in 2007. Due to their popularity and regular use as a source of strength, these volumes have been combined into one volume that best suits readers' needs.

Originally, these prayers and inspirational readings were gathered, compiled, and reimagined from various meetings, AA resources, spiritual texts, and life experiences to assist members of all Twelve Step fellowships with their prayer life and spiritual progress. In this compiled version, the prayers have been organized by the Step they best complement. The material can be read one prayer at a time for daily support or leveraged by Step or theme.

Those of you who are just beginning a life of recovery will find help with working the Twelve Steps. You may find it helpful, as you progress through the Steps, to approach this book as a daily reader, reflecting upon a prayer each day while you work a Step.

Those of you who have time in the program may want to explore the themes and Steps as needed. Those with experience know that each Step has its lessons. Now you may access the lessons and spiritual principles of each Step whenever you need to. The contents list and the following explanation of groups of the Steps will help you in selecting a specific Step and theme.

Recovery's Chapters

Every tale of recovery grapples with the same subjects: a Higher Power's presence, pursuit of self-actualization, and a renewal of relationships. There are times that your faith might waver, your forgiveness might wander, and your recovery might weaken. Pay attention always to the story you write today. Fortunately, you are blessed each day with a new start and a new story.

Steps One through Three

These Steps mark your retreat from addiction toward a complete trust in a Higher Power as you understand It. You will find your faith here, through which you will find salvation. With a Higher Power, you will write each day with grace.

Steps Four through Seven

Poisonous habits, beliefs, and despair were picked up in addiction, and they may be dropped now in recovery. Face yourself honestly, acknowledge and give away your vices, and quit yourself from addiction. With truth, you will write each day with integrity.

Steps Eight and Nine

If you seek a new life, you must face up to and atone for the old. You can heal the pain of the past with your newfound peace. With redemption, you will write each day anew.

Steps Ten through Twelve

Here lie our new codes. Steps Ten, Eleven, and Twelve ensure a perpetual involvement with our new constitution: we continually elevate ourselves, our Higher Power, and our community. If we remain watchful, we will tell a proper tale across thousands of vibrant, peaceful chapters.

In addition to reorganizing the readings by these Steps, as the original *12 Step Prayer Book* volumes 1 and 2 merged, every effort was made to determine the source of each prayer and reading included in this combined third edition. Many prayers are attributed to unknown sources. In our search for proper attribution, many of the prayers' origins could not be ascertained. While this may mean that the authors wrote them, it may also mean that the authors adapted and revised content that we were unable to find. "Source Unknown" means that we were incapable of distinguishing which scenario was more likely the case. At the very back of the book, you will find the List of Readings and Attributions that credits the source for each prayer. The list also serves as an index, providing the page number where you can locate that prayer in this book.

As you read these prayers, slogans, and stories, it will become apparent that the authors wrote with a Judeo-Christian focus. We, in no way, seek to promote or isolate any religion or spiritual belief. We welcome and celebrate a diversity of opinion, belief, and ideology. However, given the history behind these spiritual texts, we have left untouched the traditional descriptors of a Higher Power, or God, as He/Him/His.

However *you* define your Higher Power, may this collection be of assistance to you in your healing tale of recovery.

Opening Prayer

Desiderata

Go placidly amid the noise and haste, and remember what peace there may be in silence. As far as possible, without surrender, be on good terms with all persons. Speak your truth quietly and clearly; and listen to others, even the dull and ignorant; they, too, have their story.

Avoid loud and aggressive persons; they are vexations to the spirit. If you compare yourself with others, you may become vain and bitter; for always there will be greater and lesser persons than yourself. Enjoy your achievements as well as your plans.

Keep interested in your own career, however humble; it is a real possession in the changing fortunes of time. Exercise caution in your business affairs; for the world is full of trickery. But let this not blind you to what virtue there is; many persons strive for high ideals; and everywhere life is full of heroism.

Be yourself. Especially, do not feign affection. Neither be cynical about love; for in the face of all aridity and disenchantment it is perennial as the grass.

Take kindly the counsel of the years, gracefully surrendering the things of youth. Nurture strength of spirit to shield you in sudden misfortune. But do not distress yourself with dark imaginings. Many fears are born of fatigue and loneliness. Beyond a wholesome discipline, be gentle with yourself.

You are a child of the universe, no less than the trees and the stars; you have a right to be here. And whether or not it is clear to you, no doubt the universe is unfolding as it should.

Therefore be at peace with God, whatever you conceive Him to be, and whatever your labors and aspirations, in the noisy confusion of life, keep peace with your soul.

With all its sham, drudgery, and broken dreams, it is still a beautiful world. Be cheerful. Strive to be happy.

DAYBREAK

❖

Prayers to Start Your Day
with Intentionality and Mindfulness

PEACE AND GRATITUDE

·

PRESENCE

·

SAFETY

·

COMMITMENT

·

MEETINGS

·

MY RECOVERY

Your day will grow gently if you are present.

For Another Day

Thank You, dear God, for another day,
The chance to live in a decent way,
To feel again the joy of living,
And happiness that comes from giving.
Thank You for friends who can understand
And the peace that flows from Your loving hand.
Help me to wake to the morning sun
With the prayer, "Today Thy will be done,"
For with Your help I will find the way.
Thank You again, dear God, for another day.

A Peaceful Pace

Today, God, help me focus on a peaceful pace rather than a harried one. I will keep moving forward gently, not frantically. Help me let go of my need to be anxious, upset, and harried. Help me replace it with a need to be at peace and in harmony.

Every Morning

Every morning I will rest my arms awhile upon the windowsill of heaven, gaze upon my Higher Power, and with that vision in my heart, turn strong to meet my day.

O God of Our Understanding

This is the dawn of a new day in the program. I shall thank You, my Higher Power, for last night's rest, Your gift.

Yesterday is gone, except for what I have learned from it, good or bad. Today I have the same choice, a Divine privilege which swells my heart with hope and purpose. This is my day, the purity of a new beginning.

I will receive from this day exactly what I give to it. As I do good things, good will be done to me. It is my gift to mold into something everlasting and to do those things that will affect the people around me in an ever-widening circle. The worthiness of this effort rests entirely with me.

This is my day for love, because I know that as I love, I will be loved. Hate and jealousy cannot exist in the presence of love. I will be sustained by this miracle of Your creation and this day will be lightened by my love for others and especially love for my fellow travelers in the program.

Today I will do my best without thought of failures of the past or anxieties for the future. When this day is ended, I will have no regrets. On retiring I shall thank You, my Higher Power, for this wonderful day.

A Morning Prayer

Good morning, God. You are ushering in another day,
    all nice and freshly new.
Here I come again, dear Lord. Please renew me too.
Forgive the many errors that I made yesterday
And let me come again, dear God,
    to walk in Your own way.
But, God, You know I cannot do it on my own.
Please take my hand and hold it tight,
    for I cannot walk alone.

May I Be Happy

I will sit down, quiet my mind, and connect with that
which is greater than my small self and pray:

May I be free from fear.

May I be free from suffering.

May I be free from my ego.

May I be filled with loving-kindness.

May I be happy.

Time Somebody Told Me

Time somebody told me
That I am lovely, good, and real.
That my beauty could make hearts stand still.

Time somebody told me
That my love is total and so complete,
That my mind is quick and full of wit,
That my loving is just too good to quit.

Time somebody told me
How much a person wants, loves, and needs me,
How much my spirit helps set that person free,
How my eyes shine full of the white light,
How good it feels just to hold me tight.
Time somebody told me.

So I had a talk with myself,
Just me, nobody else,
'Cause it *was* time somebody told me.

Fear No More

I will not fear those who have hurt me,
For You have given me power.
I shall sleep without nightmares;
You have given me peace.
I shall awaken with a clear and rested mind;
You have given me clarity.
I shall start my day happy, joyous, and free;
You have given me my recovery;
You have given me a new life.
For Your grace,
I will demonstrate my gratitude
In useful and positive action
Throughout this day.

Quiet Day

This is another day, O Lord.
I don't know what it will bring
    for I have not scheduled anything.
If I am to sit still,
    help me to sit quietly.
If I am to rest,
    help me rest patiently.
And if I am to do nothing,
    help me do it serenely.
For it is Your will
    for me to be comfortably quiet.

Praised Be You, My Lord

Praised be You, my Lord, through our Sister
Mother Earth, who sustains us, governs us, and
Who produces varied fruits with colored flowers.

Praised be You, my Lord, through Brother Wind
And through the air, cloudy and serene, and
Every kind of weather.

Praised be You, my Lord, through Sister Moon and
The stars in heaven; You formed them clear and
Precious and beautiful.

Praised be You, my Lord, through Brother Fire,
Through whom You light the night.

Praised be You, my Lord, with all Your creatures,
Especially Sir Brother Sun, who is the day and
Through whom You give us light. And He is
Beautiful and radiant with great splendors and bears
Likeness to You, Most High One.

Happiness

Happiness is not a matter of good fortune or worldly possessions. It's a mental attitude. It comes from appreciating what we have, instead of being miserable about what we don't have. It's so simple—yet so difficult for the human mind to comprehend.

On Awakening

God, please direct my thinking; especially move it from self-pity, dishonest, and self-seeking motives.

As I go through the day and face indecision, please give me the inspiration, an intuitive thought, or a decision. Make me relax and take it easy; don't let me struggle. Let me rely upon Your inspiration, intuitive thoughts, and decision instead of my old ideas.

Show me all through the day what my next step is to be, and give me whatever I need to take care of each problem. God, I ask You especially for freedom from self-will, and I make no requests for myself only. But give me the knowledge of Your will for me and the power to carry it out in every contact during the day.

As I go through this day, let me pause when agitated or doubtful and ask You for the right thought or action. Let me constantly be reminded that I am no longer running the show, humbly saying many times each day, "Thy will be done," and agreeing that it is.

I will then be in much less danger of excitement, fear, anger, worry, self-pity, or foolish decisions. I will be more efficient. I won't be burning up energy foolishly as I was when trying to run life to suit myself. I will let You discipline me in this simple way. I will give You all the responsibility and all the praise.

This Day

This is the day which the Lord has made;
let us rejoice and be glad in it.

Run the Race

Help me this day, Higher Power, to run with patience the race that is set before me.

May neither opposition without nor discouragement within divert me from my progress in recovery.

Inspire in me strength of mind, willingness, and acceptance, that I may meet all fears and difficulties with courage and may complete the tasks set before me today.

One More Day

We carry the solution within us.
All that comes our way is blessed.
The Great Spirit gives us one more day.
We silence our fearful mind.

Do not wait to open our hearts.
Let us flow with the Mystery.
Sometimes the threads have no weave.
The price of not loving ourselves is high.

Just for Today

Just for today I will try to live through this day only, and not tackle my whole life problem at once. I can do something for twelve hours that would appall me if I felt that I had to keep it up for a lifetime.

Just for today I will be happy. This assumes to be true what Abraham Lincoln said, that "most folks are as happy as they make their minds to be."

Just for today I will try to strengthen my mind. I will study; I will learn something useful; I will not be a mental loafer; I will read something that requires effort, thought, and concentration.

Just for today I will have a program. I may not follow it exactly, but I will have it. I will save myself from two pests: hurry and indecision.

Just for today I will have a quiet half hour all by myself, and relax. During this half hour, sometime, I will try to get a better perspective on my life.

Just for today I will be unafraid. I will enjoy that which is beautiful, and will believe that as I give to the world, so the world will give to me.

Take Time

Today I pray that I can:

Take time to think.
    It is the source of power.
Take time to play.
    It is the secret of perpetual youth.
Take time to read.
    It is the fountain of wisdom.
Take time to pray.
    It is the greatest power on earth.
Take time to be friendly.
    It is the road to happiness.
Take time to laugh.
    It is the music of the soul.
Take time to give.
    It is too short a day to be selfish.
Take time to work.
    It is the price of success.
Take time to do charity.
    It is the key to heaven.

Celtic Morning Prayer

This morning, as I kindle the fire upon my hearth,
I pray that the flame of God's love may burn in my heart,
and the hearts of all I meet today.

I pray that no envy or anger, no hatred or fear, may
smother the flame.

I pray that indifference and apathy, contempt and pride,
may not pour like cold water on the fire.

Instead, may the spark of God's love light the love in
my heart, that it may burn brightly throughout the day.

And may I warm those who are lonely, whose hearts
are cold and lifeless, so that all may know the comfort
of God's love.

With Laughter

O God, as the day returns and brings us the silly
    rounds of irritating duties, help me perform them
    with laughter and a kind face.
Let cheerfulness overflow in my work;
Give me joy during my business all this day;
Bring me to my resting bed tired and content and
    grant me the gift of sleep.

My Work Life

Today, I will pay attention to what recovery behaviors I could practice that would improve my work life. I will take care of myself on the job. God, help me let go of my need to be victimized by work. Help me be open to all the good stuff that is available to me through work.

Then and Now

That was then—when my heart was drawn to evil.
Every moment was a trap waiting for me.
Every word spoken was a lie and hurtful.
I felt only sadness and pain.
My eyes saw nothing but darkness.
My days were filled with despair and doubt.

This is now—my heart is filled with Your love.
Every moment offers new opportunity.
Words spoken are truthful and kind.
I feel joy and warmth.
I awaken to another beautiful day.
My days are filled with faith and hope.

Life Is a Celebration

Lord, help me today to:

Mend a quarrel.
Seek out a forgotten friend.
Dismiss suspicion and replace it with trust.
Write a friendly letter.
Give a soft answer.
Encourage another.
Manifest my loyalty in word and deed.
Keep a promise.
Find the time.
Forgive an enemy.
Acknowledge any wrongdoing.
Try to understand.
Examine my demands on others.
Think of someone else first.
Be kind.
Be gentle.
Laugh a little.
Be happy.
Show my gratitude.
Speak Your love.
Speak it again.

Life is a celebration!

My Bill of Rights

I have the right to be treated with respect.
I have the right to say no and not feel guilty.
I have the right to experience and express my feelings.
I have the right to take time for myself.
I have the right to change my mind.
I have the right to ask for what I want.
I have the right to ask for information.
I have the right to make mistakes.
I have the right to do less than I am humanly capable of.
I have the right to feel good about myself.
I have the right to act only in ways that promote my
    dignity and self-respect as long as others are not
    violated in the process.

Sleepless Nights

Thank You, Father, that the longest night ends in dawn
and a new day.
Thank You, that Your mercies are new every morning.
Clear from my mind now all black thoughts of the
night and give me confidence as I face today.
Give me strength in my tiredness and the sure hope
that Your love will guard and keep me.

Protected and Safe

Dear God, help me feel protected and safe today.
Free my mind from resentment, doubt, and fear
 and fill me with love, peace, and hope.
When my faith in You and the Twelve Steps
 and the fellowship is strong,
 I feel protected against the storms of life
 and safe in my mind and home.

The Secret

I met God in the morning
When my day was at its best,
And His presence came like sunrise,
Like a glory in my breast.

All day long this presence lingered,
All day long He stayed with me,
And we sailed in perfect calmness
O'er a very troubled sea.

Other ships were torn and battered;
Other ships were sore distressed;
But the winds that seemed to drive them
Brought me to a peace and rest.

Then I thought of other mornings
With a keen remorse of mind,
When I, too, had loosed the moorings
With this presence left behind.

So I think I've found the secret
Learned through many a troubled way:
You must meet God in the morning
If you want Him through the day.

I Didn't Have Time

I got up early one morning
And rushed right into the day.
I had so much to accomplish
That I didn't have time to pray.
Problems just tumbled about me
And heavier came each task.
"Why doesn't God help me?" I wondered.
He answered, "You didn't ask."
I wanted to see joy and beauty
But the day toiled on, gray and bleak.
I wondered why God didn't show me.
He said, "But you didn't seek."
I tried to come into God's presence;
I used all my keys at the lock.
God gently and lovingly chided,
"My child, you didn't knock."
I woke up early this morning
And paused before entering the day.
I had so much to accomplish
That I had to take time to pray.

I Will Attend a Meeting

Creator, I will attend a meeting today.
I promise to seek out the similarities and not the
    differences.
I will find something good in everything that is shared.
I will praise the clean and sober and pray for the using
    addict.
At the end of the day I will thank You for my recovery.
It does not matter if the meeting was good or bad.
The most important thing is that I was there.

Meeting Prayer No. 1

Our Father, we come to you as a friend.

You have said that, where two or three are gathered
in Your name, there You will be in the midst.
We believe You are with us now.

We believe this is something You would have us do,
and that it has Your blessing.

We believe that You want us to be real partners with
You in this business of living, accepting our full
responsibility and certain that the rewards will be
freedom, and growth, and happiness.

For this, we are grateful.

We ask You, at all times, to guide us.

Help us daily to come closer to you, and grant us new
ways of living our gratitude.

Meeting Prayer No. 2

Our Heavenly Father, we ask for Your blessings on this
    meeting.

Please bless the spirit and the purpose of this group,

Give us strength to follow this program according to
    Your will and in all humility.

Forgive us for yesterday, and grant us courage for today
    and hope for tomorrow.

Meeting Prayer No. 3

God, bless this meeting and the members gathered here tonight.

Help us to make this group a haven of strength and comfort, giving to all who seek help here the beauty and friendliness of home, which shall be as a shield against temptation of all kinds and against loneliness and despair.

Bless those who are going forth from this house to fight the gallant fight, to know suffering; and bless those who come here to rest, those who must readjust themselves to face life once more.

Through These Doors

Dear God,
Please get me through these doors.
A meeting is what I need.
Remind me to leave my ego and intolerance outside.
Help me to hear the strength and hope in everyone's
    words.
We are the same but appear so different.
I will remember that others' experiences will help my
    recovery just as my experience may help another.

My Medallion

I always carry my medallion,
A simple reminder to me
Of the fact that I'm in recovery
No matter where I may be.

This little chip is not magic
Nor is it a good luck charm.
It isn't supposed to protect me
From every possible harm.

It's not meant for comparison,
Or for all the world to see,
It's simply an understanding
Between my Higher Power and me.

Whenever I doubt the cost
I paid for recovery,
I look at my medallion
To remember what used to be.

Anniversary Prayer

Dear God,

I had another anniversary today, one more year in recovery. It has been difficult at times, but it has allowed many blessings. I am a human being again. I feel new strength in my body, spirit, and mind. The world has never looked so good. I have the respect of my friends and family. I am productive in my work. I do not miss the slippery people and places. When I have been tempted, You, my Higher Power, have sustained me. I have found a home in the fellowship and friends who support me. Stay close by me, God. I thank You. This is the life I love.

STEP ONE

❖

Honesty and Beginnings

BEGIN

·

TURN AWAY

·

POWERLESSNESS

·

AN UNCERTAIN JOURNEY

·

TOWARD GOD

We need help.
We might not believe, yet,
And that is okay.
We are but little.

First Step Prayer

Today, I ask for help with my addiction. Denial has kept me from seeing how powerless I am and how my life is unmanageable. I need to learn and remember that I have an incurable illness and that abstinence is the only way to deal with it.

One Day at a Time

One day at a time—this is enough.
Do not look back and grieve over the past, for it is gone.
And do not be troubled about the future, for it has not
    yet come.
Live in the present, and make it so beautiful that it will
    be worth remembering.

Yesterday, Today, Tomorrow

There are two days in every week about which we should not worry, two days that should be kept free from fear and apprehension.

One of these days is *yesterday*, with its mistakes and cares, its faults and blunders, its aches and pains. *Yesterday* has passed forever beyond our control.

All the money in the world cannot bring back *yesterday*. We cannot undo a single act we performed; we cannot erase a single word we said. *Yesterday* is gone.

The other day we should not worry about is *tomorrow*, with its possible adversaries, its burdens, its large and poor performance. *Tomorrow* is also beyond our immediate control.

Tomorrow's sun will rise, either in splendor or behind a mask of clouds—but it will rise. Until it does, we have no stake in *tomorrow*, for it is as yet unborn.

This leaves only one day: *today*. Any person can fight the battle of just one day. It is only when you and I add the *yesterday* and *tomorrow* that we break down.

It is not the experience of *today* that drives people mad—it is remorse or bitterness for something that happened *yesterday* and the dread of what *tomorrow* may bring.

Let us, therefore, live but one day at a time!

Blaming the Past

O Lord, help me stop blaming the factors that I think contributed to my addiction: parents, relatives, friends, the church, and most important, myself. Help me realize that understanding may be helpful, but blaming is always counterproductive. The program teaches that the reasons are not that important. My progress and growth in recovery are based on the spiritual. God, help me focus on how Your Spirit, in me and through me, guides me away from blaming the past.

Lead Me from Addiction

Lead me from addiction, in thought and action, to life,
From falsehood to truth.
Lead me from despair to hope,
From fear to trust.
Lead me from resentment to acceptance,
From hate to love.
Let peace fill my heart,
Let serenity be my goal,
This I pray.

I Am Weak

Lord, I am feeling weak—hear my prayer.
Lord, keep me from turning away from You.
I don't want to go back under.
Let me hear Your voice and feel Your faithful love.
I put my trust in You, Lord.
Keep me from my addiction; show me the way.
Teach me Your will.

Change Me

Change me, God,
Please change me.
Though I cringe
Kick
Resist and resent.
Pay no attention to me whatsoever.
When I run to hide
Drag me out of my safe little shelter.
Change me totally.
Whatever it takes.
However long You must work at the job.
Change me—and save me
From spiritual self-destruction.

Grant Me Your Light

Just for today,
What does it matter, O Lord, if the future is dark?
To pray now for tomorrow—I am not able.
Keep my heart only for today,
Give me Your protection today,
Grant me your light—
Just for today.

This First Step

Lord, I have nothing.
My addiction has taken my spirit and my sanity.
I have lost my family and my soul.
My life is no longer my own.
Help me to restore my life so it is manageable;
Make my pains bearable.
I cannot do it alone—I have tried.
Today I ask that You will be with me
    as I take this First Step.

Breton Fisherman's Prayer

Dear God, be good to me.
The sea is so wide, and my boat is so small.

No Standing Still

Spirit of the Universe, never let me think that I have knowledge enough to need no teaching, wisdom enough to need no correction, talents enough to need no grace, goodness enough to need no progress, humility enough to need no repentance, devotion enough to need no inspiration, strength sufficient without Your Spirit; fearing, if I stand still, I will fall back for evermore.

Help

Dear God, this I pray:

Help me until I can trust my own thoughts,
Encourage me until I regain my self-esteem,
Love me until I am able to love myself,
Protect me from my demons until I can fight them
    with You.

God, Help Me Live Today

God, more than anything else in this world, I just don't
    want to be sick anymore.
If You please, Lord, free me enough of the bondage of
    self that I may be of some useful value as a human
    being, whether I understand or not,
That I may carry my own keys, maintain my own
    integrity, and live this day at peace with You,
    at peace with myself, and at peace with the world
    I live in, just for today.
God help me during this day to demonstrate that,
    in the spirit of St. Francis of Assisi,
It is good for me to love and to be loved.
It is good for me to understand and to be understood.
It is good for me to give and to receive.
It is good for me to comfort and to allow myself to be
    comforted.
And it is obviously far better for me to be useful as a
    human being than it is to be selfish.
God, help me please to put one foot in front of the
    other, to keep moving forward, and to do the best
    I can with what I have to work with today,
Accepting the results of whatever that may
    or may not be.

Don't Quit

When things go wrong as they sometimes will,
When the road you're trudging seems all uphill,
When the funds are low and the debts are high,
And you want to smile, but you have to sigh;
When care is pressing you down a bit,
Rest, if you must, but don't quit.
Life is funny with its twists and turns,
As every one of us sometimes learns;
And many a failure has turned about
When they might have won had they stuck it out.
Don't give up though the pace seems slow;
You may succeed with another blow.
Success is failure turned inside out:
The silver tint of the clouds of doubt.
And you can never tell how close you are;
It may be near when it seems so far.
So stick to the fight when you're hardest hit.
It's when things seem worst that you must not quit.

Farther Along

Tempted and tried, we're often made to wonder
Why it should be like this all day long,
While there are other addicts using among us,
Never paying consequences though in the wrong.

Farther along we'll know all about it;
Farther along we'll understand why.
Cheer up my fellow travelers;
Live in the sunshine.
We'll understand it all, by and by.

Sometimes I wonder why I must struggle,
Go in the rain, the cold, and the snow
When there are many living in comfort
Giving no heed to all I can do.

Faithful till death, said our loving Master;
Short is our time to labor and wait;
Then will our toiling seem to be nothing
When we shall pass the heavenly gate.

Farther along we'll know all about it;
Farther along we'll understand why.
Cheer up my brother;
Live in the sunshine.
We'll understand it all, by and by.

The Right Road

Dear God,
I have no idea where I am going.
I do not see the road ahead of me.
I cannot know for certain where it will end.
Nor do I really know myself, and the fact that I am
    actually doing so.
But I believe this.
I believe that the desire to please You does in fact
    please You.
I hope I have that desire in everything I do.
I hope I never do anything apart from that desire.
And I know that if I do this, You will lead me by the
    right road though I may know nothing about it at
    the time.
Therefore, I will trust You always, for though I may
    seem to be lost, and in the shadow of death, I will
    not be afraid, because I know You will never leave
    me to face my troubles alone.

Strengthen Me

Lord, I am an empty vessel that needs to be filled.
My Lord, fill it.
I am weak in faith; strengthen me.
I am cold in love; warm me and make me enthusiastic—
That my love may go out to my neighbor.
I do not have a strong and firm faith;
At times I doubt and am unable to trust you.
O Lord, help me.
Strengthen my faith and trust in You.

You Give Me Strength

Lord God, thank You for loving me
Even when I turn away from You.
I am grateful for Your constant care and concern.
Though I feel unworthy of Your great love,
I thank You that through my weakness
You give me strength,
And in my wanderings You show me the way.

A Beginner's Prayer

Lord, I want to love You, yet I am not sure.
I want to trust You, yet I am afraid of being taken in.
I know I need You, but I am ashamed of the need.
I want to pray, but I am afraid of being a hypocrite.
I need my independence, yet I fear to be alone.
I want to belong, yet I must be myself.
Take me, Lord, yet leave me alone.
Lord, I believe; help me with my unbelief.
O Lord, if You are there, You do understand,
    don't You?
Give me what I need, but leave me free to choose.
Help me work it out my own way, but don't let me go.
Let me understand myself, but don't let me despair.
Come unto me, O Lord, I want You there.
Lighten my darkness, but don't dazzle me.
Help me to see what I need to do, and give me
    strength to do it.
O Lord, I believe; help me with my unbelief.

Grant Me to Walk in Beauty

I come before You as one of Your Children.
See, I am small and weak;
I pray for Your strength and wisdom.
Grant me to walk in beauty and that my eyes may
    ever behold the crimson sunset.
May my hands treat with respect
    the things that You have created;
May my ears hear Your voice.

Make me wise, that I may understand the things
    that You have taught others in our program.
I long for strength, not that I may outreach others,
    but to fight my greatest enemy—myself.

Make me ever ready to come to You with clear
    thinking and candid eyes, so that my spirit,
    when life disappears like the setting sun, may
    stand unashamed before You.

Attitude and Outlook

God, help me to work on a positive attitude and outlook in my life. Help me adapt to the real world no matter how different and difficult it seems. During my addiction, I tried to escape reality and live in a world of fantasy. Recovery has taught me I can't change the facts of living, but I can change my attitude toward them. Today, I will learn new attitudes toward life's challenges and practice new solutions by working the program. I'm learning to live in the real world with a healthy attitude and outlook.

Finding Home

Dear God, help me think of . . .
Stepping on shore, and finding it Heaven!
Taking a hand, and finding it God's hand.
Breathing new air, and finding it celestial air.
Feeling invigorated, and finding it immortality.
Passing from storm and tempest to an unbroken calm.
Waking up, and finding it Home.

STEP TWO

✤

Hope and Belief

FAITH WAVERS

·

FAITH GROWS

·

BELIEVING RESOLUTION

We are addicted, and it is unmanageable—
There is no shame in this.
We look toward our Higher Power
And learn to believe.

Second Step Prayer

I pray for an open mind so I may come to believe in a Power greater than myself. I pray for humility and the continued opportunity to increase my faith. I don't want to be crazy anymore.

The Letter

How are you? I just had to send a note to tell you how much I care about you.

I saw you yesterday as you were talking with your friends. I waited all day hoping you would want to talk to me too. I gave you a sunset to close your day and a cool breeze to rest you—and I waited. You never came. It hurt me, but I still love you because I am your friend.

I saw you sleeping last night and longed to touch your brow, so I spilled moonlight upon your face. Again I waited, wanting to rush down so we could talk. I have so many gifts for you! You awoke and rushed off to work. My tears were in the rain.

If you would only listen to me! I love you! I try to tell you in blue skies and in the quiet green grass. I whisper it in leaves on the trees and breathe it in colors of flowers, shout it to you in mountain streams, give the birds love songs to sing. My love for you is deeper than the ocean and bigger than the biggest need in your heart!

Ask me! Talk to me! Please don't forget me. I have so much to share with you!

I won't hassle you any further. It is your decision. I have chosen you, and I will wait.

I love you.
Your friend,
God

Lack of Faith

Dear God, help me to stop demanding maturity without the pains of experience and growth. It is both unreasonable and impossible. I need faith in the process to reach maturity. Lack of faith arrests my progress in recovery. Procrastination and skepticism are enemies of spiritual progress and attainment.

Skepticism demands evidence of God's help. Procrastination prevents it. Faith, willingness, and prayer overcome all obstacles and provide ample evidence of God's help in our happy, clean, and sober lives.

When I Question God's Will

There are still times when I feel insecure and uneasy about my life. At those times, I question Your will for me. I wonder if I'm being punished for something I have done wrong or if I'm not working the program hard enough. I must hold fast to the truth that I am just where You would have me. I must stop taking control and attempting to force changes I'm not ready for. This is when I lose touch with You. I will be patient and believe answers will emerge at exactly the right time.

Footprints

One night a man had a dream. He dreamed he was walking along the beach with the Lord. Across the sky flashed scenes from his life. For each scene, he noticed two sets of footprints in the sand: one belonging to him, and the other to the Lord.

When the last scene of his life flashed before him, he looked back at the footprints in the sand. He noticed that many times along the path of his life there was only one set of footprints. He also noticed that it happened at the very lowest and saddest times in his life.

This really bothered him, and he questioned the Lord about it. "Lord, You said that once I decided to follow You, You'd walk with me all the way. But I have noticed that during the most troublesome times in my life, there is only one set of footprints. I don't understand why, when I needed You most, You would leave me."

The Lord replied, "My precious, precious child, I love you and I would never leave you. During your times of trial and suffering, when you see only one set of footprints, it was then that I carried you."

Prayer during Turmoil

Dear Higher Power,
During times when my world becomes unhinged
And the foundations of what I believe crack and
    dissolve,
Give me the grace to believe that Your power is at
    work in the turmoil of my life.
Lead me to remember that Your power is greater than
    all evil,
And though the world may rock and sometimes break,
It will in time be transformed by Your Love.

Faith Works

God, help me look beyond material things
And place my faith in the unseen.
For faith saves me from despair
For faith saves me from worry and care
For faith brings peace beyond all understanding
For faith brings me all the strength I need
For faith gives me a new vital power
And a wonderful peace and serenity.

Rejecting Rejection

"God don't make junk." In other words, every person has an infinite spiritual worth that has nothing to do with the ordinary judgments of the marketplace and the world. Other people may reject us for both good and bad reasons, but the real Source of our existence will never turn us away.

Moreover, this Higher Power is also capable of leading each of us to the people and places that fit our needs and our social talents for service. Many of us who are now in recovery feel that this happened when we were being led to the fellowship.

Blessed St. Teresa's Prayer

Let nothing upset you;
Let nothing frighten you.
Everything is changing;
God alone is changeless.
Patience attains the goal.
Who has God lacks nothing:
God alone fills all of our needs.

We Need Only Obey

Dear God, I realize the whole course of things goes to teach me faith. I need only obey. There is guidance for me, and by listening I shall hear the right word. I will place myself in the middle of the stream of power and wisdom that flows from You; I will place myself in the center of that flood. And then I may know the truth, the right, and contentment.

Faith

Faith is a knowledge within the heart, beyond the reach of proof.

God's Power to Guide Me

I arise today
Through a mighty strength:

God's power to guide me,
God's might to uphold me,
God's wisdom to teach me,
God's eyes to watch me,
God's ear to hear me,
God's word to give me speech,
God's hand to guard me,
God's way to lie before me,
God's shield to shelter me,
God's host to secure me:
    Against the snares of devils,
    Against the seductions of vices,
    Against the lusts of nature,
    Against everyone who shall wish me ill,
    Whether far or near, many or few.

Teach Me

Dear God, teach me
    to listen to Your many blessings.
Steer my life toward Your will
    and the tranquil haven You provide
    for all storm-tossed souls.
Show me the course I should take.
Renew a willing spirit within me.
Let Your spirit curb my wayward senses.
Enable me unto that which is my true good:
    to keep Your laws and, in all my works,
    to rejoice in Your glorious presence.

Make Us Strong

O our Father, the Sky,
    hear us and make us strong.
O our Mother, the Earth,
    hear us and give us support.
O Spirit of the East,
    send us Your wisdom.
O Spirit of the South,
    may we tread Your path.
O Spirit of the West,
    may we always be ready for the long journey.
O Spirit of the North,
    purify us with Your cleansing winds.

Accepting Every Task

Dear God, help me find the strength to be effective and accept responsibility. I am asking You for the strength I need each day. You have proven in countless lives that for every day I live, You will give me that necessary power. I must face every challenge that comes to me during the day sure that You will give me the strength to face it. I pray that I may accept every task as a challenge. I know I cannot wholly fail if You are with me.

To Be Useful

Thank You, God, for I am glad to be useful, to have a reason for living, to have a purpose in life.

I want to lose my life in this wonderful fellowship and so find it again.

I need the Twelve Step principles for the development of the buried life within me, the good life I misplaced before the program.

Thank You, God, for this recovery life within me is growing slowly but surely, with setbacks and mistakes, but still developing. I cannot yet know what it will be, but I know it will be good. That's all I want to know. It will be good.

Life Is a Gift

Thank you, God. May I remember during periods of depression,

The many times in my life when things do seem right, when I have those moments of clarity,

When I feel there is hope, when the sun shines down on me and warms my face, when Your love warms my heart.

I am reminded that life is a gift . . . this I pray.

The Way

Dear Lord, today I pray:

The way is long;
Let us go together.

The way is difficult;
Let us help each other.

The way is joyful;
Let us share it.

The way is ours alone;
Let us go in love.

The way grows before us;
Let us begin.

A Useful Life

My Creator, You have examined my heart
   and know everything about me.
You chart the path ahead of me,
   and tell me where to stop and rest.
Every moment, You know where I am.
You know what I am going to say before I say it.
This is too glorious, too wonderful to believe!
I can never be lost to Your Spirit!
I can never get away from my God!
If I ride the morning winds to the farthest oceans,
   even there Your hand will guide me,
   Your strength will support me.

Search me, O God, and know my heart.
Test my thoughts;
Point out anything You find in me
   that makes You sad, and lead me along
   the path of a useful life.

This I Believe

Tomorrow is yet to be,
But should God grant me another day,
The hope, courage, and strength
Through the working of the Twelve Steps and Serenity
    Prayer,
I shall be sufficiently provided for to meet my every
    need.
This I believe.

An Irish Blessing

May the road rise to meet you,
May the wind be always at your back,
May the sun shine warm upon your face,
The rain fall softly on your fields,
And until we meet again,
May God hold you in the palm of His hand.

A Triumphant Heart

Give us, O Lord, a tireless heart,
So no false accusation may drag us down.
Give us a triumphant heart,
So no hardship can wear us out;
Give us an honest heart,
So no unworthy thought may tempt us.
Grant upon us also, Our Creator,
Understanding to know You,
Persistence to seek You,
Wisdom to find You,
And faithfulness that we may embrace You.

Who Are You to Say There Is No God?

As I reflected on this question I tumbled out of bed
    to my knees.

I am overwhelmed by a conviction of the Presence
    of God.

It pours through me with the certainty and majesty
    of a great tide at flood.

The barriers I have built denying Your Spirit through
    the years are swept away.

I stand now in the presence of Your Infinite Power
    and Love.

I have stepped from bridge to shore.

For the first time, I live in conscious companionship
    with my Creator.

STEP THREE

❖

Faith and Commitment

NEEDING GOD

·

SLOW TRUST

·

BONDAGE OF SELF

·

COMPLETE SURRENDER

Through our Higher Power, all things are possible.
But faith is little without action.
We surrender ourselves entirely
To a spiritual direction.

Third Step Prayer

God, I offer myself to Thee—to build with me and to do
with me as Thou wilt. Relieve me of the bondage of self,
that I may better do Thy will. Take away my difficulties,
that victory over them may bear witness to those I would
help of Thy Power, Thy Love, and Thy Way of life. May
I do Thy will always!

Father of Light

O my Father, Father of Light,
Who watches over us all,
I have no words to thank You.
But with Your great wisdom
I am sure that You can see
My willingness to change
And how I value Your glorious gifts.

O my Father, when I look upon Your greatness,
I am confounded with awe.
O Supreme Being,
Ruler of all things earthly and heavenly,
I am your warrior,
Ready to act in accordance with Your will.

Surround Me with Your Love, God

Surround me with Your love and guidance, O God;
I am not safe without You.
I am constantly exposed to this stressful world.
I am in danger sometimes of losing the battle to the
    very shortcomings of my own nature.
I can only surrender myself to You
    and believe that You will fulfill Your purpose in me.

I surrender to Your will, O God,
    even when I am beaten down by depression
    and caught up by my defects
    and my own appetites threaten my recovery.
You are my God, and You will not let me go.

Your love, O God, is an answered promise.
Your wisdom is an answered prayer.

Burden No Longer

Lord, take away this ache in my heart. I know I have asked this of You before. This ache consumes my every waking moment, haunts my dreams, weakens my spirit. I pray You take this from me so the burden is no longer my own, but ours together. I have wasted enough energy and am ready to turn it over to You completely. I believe in You and Your will for me.

No Other

I have no other helper than You,
    no other father,
    no other redeemer,
    no other support.
I pray to You.
Only You can help me.
My present misery is too great.
Despair grips me, and I am at my wits' end.
I am sunk in the depths, and I cannot pull myself up
    or out.
If it is Your will, help me out of this misery.
Let me know that You are stronger than all misery and
    all enemies.
O Lord, if I come through this, let the experience
    contribute to my and my brothers' blessings.
You will not forsake me; this I know.

Use Me as Your Worker

Dear God, Your grace has placed me in recovery. You know how unstable and sick I was. Were it not for my surrender to Your guidance, the fellowship, and the program, I would have brought everything to destruction. I wish to give my heart and actions to Your service. I desire to teach Your message and be taught Your work.

God Is Doing for Us

Dear God, as I practice patience, belief, and trust in surrendering to Your will for me, I now trust that solutions and miracles come in Your time, not mine. This promise tells me I must accept Your help, not merely be resigned to it. I pray I will let go of my problems and turn them over to You with faith.

The Bike Ride

At first I saw God as my observer, my judge.

But later on, when I recognized my Higher Power, it seemed as though life was rather like a bike ride, but it was a tandem bike, and I noticed that God was in the back helping me pedal.

I don't know just when it was that He suggested we change places, but life has not been the same since . . . life with my Higher Power, that is. I did not trust Him at first, in control of my life. I thought He'd wreck it. But He knew bike secrets, knew how to make it bend to take sharp corners, jump to clear high places filled with rocks, fly to shorten scary passages.

And I'm learning to shut up and pedal in the strangest places, and I'm beginning to enjoy the view and the cool breeze on my face with my delightful constant companion, my Higher Power.

And when I'm sure I can't do anymore, He just smiles and says, *"Pedal!"*

Walk with Me

Don't walk in front of me . . . I may not follow.
Don't walk behind me . . . I may not lead.
Just walk beside me and be my friend.

Looking for God

Higher Power, I remember when I was new to recovery I was told to go out and find You. I made little progress until I realized, through surrendering my will, You had always been trying to find me. I then began to recognize the ways You are already here with me. Once I learned to feel Your presence, in my good and bad days, it became much easier to trust You and to surrender to Your will.

Help Me Remember

Lord,
Help me remember that nothing is going to happen to
me today that You and I together can't handle.

Serenity Prayer

God, grant me the serenity
to accept the things I cannot change,
courage to change the things I can,
and wisdom to know the difference.

Living one day at a time;
Enjoying one moment at a time;
Accepting hardship as the pathway to peace;
Taking, as He did, this sinful world as it is, not as I would
   have it;
Trusting that He will make all things right if I surrender
   to His will;
That I may be reasonably happy in this life, and
   supremely happy with Him forever in the next.

For Guidance

Father of light,
Give us wisdom to know You,
Intelligence to understand You,
Courage to seek You,
Patience to wait for You,
Eyes to see You,
A heart to meditate on You,
And a life to proclaim You.

Humble, Open-Minded, Willing

Into Your hands, O Lord, I praise this joy, this sorrow,
  this problem, this decision.
Into Your hands I praise each moment as it comes,
  each event You send to me.
Into Your hands I put this thing I have to do or suffer.
Into Your hands this love, this responsibility.
Into Your hands this weakness, this defect, this failure,
  this wrong thing that I have done.
And so, finally, into Your hands I place my life
  as a whole, all that I am; be it done
  according to Your will.

Traditional Prayer from Mexico

I am only a spark;
Make me a fire.
I am only a string;
Make me a lyre.
I am only a drop;
Make me a fountain.
I am only an anthill;
Make me a mountain.
I am only a feather;
Make me a wing.
I am only a rag;
Make me a king!
To demonstrate my usefulness
To You, myself, and others.

Mychal's Prayer

Lord, take me where You want me to go;
Let me meet who You want me to meet;
Tell me what You want me to say;
And
Keep me out of Your way.

My Misadventures

O Lord, save me from taking the wrong road; save me
   from repeating my past misadventures.
I have learned in recovery that a truly satisfied life is
   only possible when I live the life You want me
   to live.
When I live with You in that secret place of the Spirit,
   I know I'm on the right road.
Your will (not mine) be done.

Gentle and Soothing

Higher Power, what have I cried out for since my first
     breath, if not serenity and tranquility?
Only when I made a decision of surrendering to Your
     will did my life change.
I then made myself open
To the gentle serenity of Your peace,
To the soothing tranquility of Your love.

Thy Will Be Done

If I were to chase each particular care, each particular worry, and each particular sorrow, I would have business on hand for the rest of my life; but if I can rise into a higher state of mind, these cease to be annoyances and cares. Ninety-nine parts in a hundred of the cares of life are cured by one single salve, and that is, "Thy will be done." The moment I can say that, and let go, that moment more than ninety-nine parts in a hundred of my troubles drop away.

Peace in God's Will

My Higher Power, quicken my spirit and fix my thoughts on Your will, that I may see what You would have done and contemplate its doing without self-consciousness or inner excitement, without haste and without delay, without fear of other people's judgments or anxiety about success, knowing only that it is Your will and therefore must be done quietly, faithfully, and lovingly, for in Your will alone is my peace.

Consciousness of God

I came, at my first surrender, not only into consciousness of God but into usefulness for God and others. I was able to do, through God's help, what no one has ever been able or ever will be able to do alone, which is to supplement the all-important "why" of life with the still more important "how" of living. I was able to begin solving my own problems and, for the first time in my experience, was given the power to begin helping others. I no longer wished well to "myself alone." Dear God, I pray to surrender again today.

My New Employer

I have a new Employer. Being all powerful,
    You provide what I need if I keep close to You
    and perform Your work well.
I have become less and less interested in myself,
    my little plans and designs.
Your wisdom shows me more and more what
    I can contribute to life.

As I feel new power flow in,
    enjoy peace of mind,
    face life successfully,
    become conscious of Your presence,
    I feel less fear of today, tomorrow, and the hereafter.
I have been reborn.

My First Prayer

I surrender to Thee my entire life, O God of my understanding. I have made a mess of it, trying to run it myself. You take it, the whole thing, and run it for me, according to Your will and plan.

Surrender to God's Will

O Lord, You know what is best for me.
Let this or that be done as You please.
Give what You will,
How much You will,
When You will.

Reason for Hope

God of hope and serenity, I sing for joy because You have given me hope and serenity as I demonstrate the principles of our program in my life. My world is sometimes full of problems, yet You give me reason for hope. I have come to You today to surrender my will to Your unfailing wisdom. Give me wisdom as I go out to my places of daily life. Teach me and guide me as I deal with problems, real or imagined. Thank You. Your will (not mine) be done.

I Have No Words to Thank You

O my Father, Great Elder,
I have no words to thank you,
But with your deep wisdom
I am sure that you can see
How I value your glorious gifts.
O my Father, when I look upon your greatness,
I am confounded with awe.
O Great Elder,
Ruler of all things earthly and heavenly,
I am your warrior,
Ready to act in accordance with your will.

Our Faithful, Unchangeable Friend

How good is the God we adore,
Our faithful, unchangeable friend!
His love is as great as His power,
And knows neither limit nor end!
Our Creator, the First and the Last,
Whose Spirit shall guide us safely home:
We'll praise Him for all that is past,
We'll trust Him for all that's to come.

STEP FOUR

❖

Courage and Truth

TRUTH AND PAIN

·

OUR DEFECTS

·

A SIGHT OF CHANGE

Our pain is rooted in fear, resentment, and misdeed.
We must recognize the faults of our past,
If we wish to create a future.

Fourth Step Prayer

Dear God,
It is I who has made my life a mess. I have done it, and I cannot undo it. My mistakes are mine, and I will begin a searching and fearless moral inventory. I will write down my wrongs, but I will also include that which is good. I pray for the strength to complete the task.

When Our Hearts Are Lonely

God of life,
There are days when the burdens we carry
Hurt our shoulders and wear us down,
When the road seems dreary and endless,
The skies gray and threatening,
When our lives have no music in them
And our hearts are lonely
And our souls have lost their courage.
Flood the path with light, we ask You,
And turn our eyes to where the skies are full of promise.

Right Living

From the cowardice that dare not face new truth
From the laziness that is contented with half-truth
From the arrogance that thinks it knows all truth,
Good Lord, deliver me.

Stop My Running Away

May I remain fearless and searching in taking my inventory. This challenge has always seemed difficult—difficult in facing myself as I really am. I cannot run away from the truth or flee from my wrongdoings. Higher Power, stop me in my tracks when my misdeeds are chasing me. May I slow down, stop, and turn to face them with the most trusty weapon that the program and You have taught me: the honest truth.

To Be Honest

Higher Power, help me to be honest with myself. It is so easy to alibi, to make excuses for my shortcomings. It is so easy to blame others and circumstances as a child does. Help me to see myself honestly: a human being who needs You this day and every day. Help me to surrender my weak will to Your strength.

Light a Candle

O God of my understanding, light a candle within my heart, that I may see what is therein and remove the wreckage of the past.

Support Me with Your Power

Lord, may everything I do
    start well and finish well.
Support me with Your power.
And in Your power let me drive away all falsehood
    so truth may always triumph.

Procrastination

Higher Power, it was so easy to put things off during my addiction. I pray to remember that postponing facing up to reality is really self-pity in action. When I procrastinate about solving problems, I am only making the problems worse. Let me remember that solutions come from taking action. I pray to stop wasting precious time.

Yes or No

Higher Power, today I will remember:
When I was practicing my addiction, I lost track
Of what was right or wrong, honest or dishonest.
Pride was defended,
Anger was justified,
Lust was accepted,
Gluttony was encouraged,
Envy was normal,
Greed was there to be satisfied,
Laziness was a way of life.

In recovery I have come to recognize and rediscover
The integrity in myself by simply knowing;
What is right is what I feel good about,
What is wrong is what I feel bad about.

This I make into a simple prayer:
I will continue to live by yes and no;
Yes to everything good,
No to everything bad.

Who, Me?

I need to be forgiven, Lord, so many times a day.
So often do I stumble and fall. Be merciful, I pray.
Help me to not be critical when others' faults I see.
For so often, Lord, the same faults are in me.

Humility Prayer

Lord, I am far too much influenced by what people think of me,

Which means that I am always pretending to be either richer or smarter than I really am. Please prevent me from trying to attract attention.

Don't let me gloat over praise on the one hand and be discouraged by criticism on the other, nor let me waste time weaving the most imaginary situations in which the heroic, charming, witty person present is myself.

Show me how to be humble of heart.

Stop Fixing Others

Dear Higher Power, when I am overly dependent on others, I try to fix them. I have a real talent in pinpointing what is wrong with other people. But the very thing that enables me to see their defects most often blinds me to the same, sometimes even worse, shortcomings in myself. Help me stop fretting about others and instead focus on correcting my own character defects.

For a Sane and Sound Sex Life

Dear God, I pray for a sane and sound ideal for my sex life. I will subject each relation to this test—is it selfish or not? I ask You to mold my ideals and help me live up to them. I will remember always that my sex powers are God-given and therefore good, neither to be used lightly or selfishly, nor to be despised and loathed. I must be willing to grow toward this ideal.

I will treat sex as any other problem and ask You what I should do in each specific situation.

The right answer will come, if I want it. I earnestly pray for the right ideal, for guidance in each questionable situation, for sanity, and for strength to do the right thing.

Healthy Pride

O Lord, deliver me from false pride. Before recovery, my false pride led to grandiosity, arrogance, egotism, self-pity, misunderstanding, and fear. My misguided pride was out of control, and I thought I knew everything. In recovery, I have learned my accomplishments are not mine alone. I rely on the guidance of others and faith in my Higher Power. When I indulge in false pride, I close my mind, which desperately needs to be open. Healthy pride in my progress, if coupled with gratitude and humility, will not cause harm. Help me, Lord; remove the intellectual false pride that blocks me from others and the principles of our program.

Avoiding Gossip

God of reason, help me be faithful to
    placing principles before personalities.
Before I gossip or find fault with others,
    help me remember to ask myself:
        Is it true?
        Is it kind?
        Is it useful?
If I can't answer yes to these questions,
    I will not gossip.
Help me talk about principles, not personalities.
    This I pray.

Losing Interest in Selfish Things

God, help me choose the path away from selfish things. I came into the program an expert in dishonesty, deceit, envy, and grandiosity. Selfishness fitted me well. I was shameless in the ways I took advantage of and manipulated other people. Help me remember that selfishness and self-centeredness are a product of a sick ego. God, I must remember, every minute, that my reborn purpose in this new way of living is to help other people.

Better Relationships

I pray for the opportunity to form better relationships now that I am in recovery. The program has revealed a need to completely overhaul my attitudes about intimate and personal relations. I pray the working of the program will help me be a better partner in relationships. Most of the time I never really needed better partners. I just needed to be a better person.

Fear and Insecurity

Lord, continue to show me I don't have to fear people. When deep in my compulsions and obsessions, I was terrified of people, especially those who loved me. This new way of life has created a feeling of safety. My new friends, surroundings, and tools for living are lifesaving. Managing finances within a budget has produced far less stress. I pray for an attitude of financial responsibility in thought and action.

Live and Let Live

O Lord, we are urged to live fully, richly, and happily—to fulfill our destiny with the joy that comes from doing well at whatever we do. O Lord, it is more difficult to let live. This means accepting the right of every other person to live as he or she wishes, without my criticism and judgment. May I live life to the fullest, understanding that pure pleasure-seeking is not pleasure-finding, but that Your goodness is here to be shared. May I learn not to take over the responsibility for another adult's decisions; that is my old controlling self trying one more time to be the executive director of other people's lives. Dear God, help me to live and let live.

Bad Day

Today was a bad day.
Forgive me for my anger toward others;
The anger was my own.
Forgive me for my prejudice toward others;
The prejudice and intolerance came
  from my own arrogance.
Forgive me for my lack of faith in You;
My lack of faith is my own fear of failure.
Tomorrow will be a better day.
I had a bad day, but it has ended.
And I am sober.

We Will Not Regret the Past

My Creator, by cleaning house and taking my inventory, I have been able to honestly face myself and stop hiding from the world and myself. I am learning what kind of person I am. This is necessary for maintaining abstinence and preventing a slip. Without awareness of what the past did to me, I cannot truly carry the message of hope and the gift of recovery to those who desperately need it. God, I pray to visit my past but never live in it for long.

Letting Go

As children bring their broken toys
With tears for us to mend,
I brought my broken dreams to God,
Because God is my friend.
But then, instead of leaving my Higher Power
In peace to work alone,
I hung around and tried to help,
With ways that were my own.
At last, I snatched them back and cried,
"How can You be so slow?"
"My child," God said, "what could I do?
You never did let go."

Deliver Me from Fear

O Lord, I ask you to deliver me from
The fear of the unknown future,
The fear of failure,
The fear of poverty,
The fear of sadness,
The fear of loneliness,
The fear of sickness and pain,
The fear of age, and
The fear of death.
Help me, Higher Power, by Your grace, to love.
Fill my heart with cheerful courage
And loving trust in You.

I Must Change

Spirit of the Universe, I pray to remember.
No one can make me change.
No one can stop me from changing.
No one really knows how I must change,
Not even I. Not until I start.
Help me remember that it only takes a slight shift
In direction to begin to change my life.

Next Right Step

God, please show me all through this day,
What is the next right step.
Give me the strength, faith, and courage
I need to take care of the problems in my life.
Show me the solutions, for I will take the
Next right actions. And I ask to be free
From self-will and fear. Your will, not mine,
Be done. Amen.

STEP FIVE

❊

Integrity and Trust

A FORMING FUTURE

·

MATERIAL CHANGE

Our past and future selves meet here.
With our Higher Power,
We look back at who we became,
And begin anew.

Fifth Step Prayer

Higher Power, my inventory has shown me who I am, yet I ask for Your help in admitting my wrongs to another person and to You. Assure me, and be with me in this Step, for without this Step I cannot progress in my recovery. With Your help, I can do this, and I will do it.

Make Me Brave for Life

God, make me brave for life: Oh, braver than this.
Let me straighten after pain, as a tree straightens
    after rain,
Shining and lovely again.
God, make me brave for life, much braver than this.
As the blown grass lifts, let me rise
From sorrow with quiet eyes,
Knowing Your will is wise.
God, make me brave; life brings
Such blinding things.
Help me to keep my sight;
Help me to see what's right,
That out of dark comes light.

The Fear Prayer

God, thank You for helping me to be honest
Enough to see the truth about myself.
Thank You for showing me my fears;
Please help me remove them.
Help me outgrow my fears,
The fears that have haunted me
And blocked me from doing Your will.
Direct my attention to what You
Would have me be.
Demonstrate through me and
Help me do Your will always.

Let the Worst Be Known

Lord, this I pray:
As long as I'm preoccupied with my own secret
    problems, not sharing them with anyone,
I'm critical, insensitive, selfish, and full of self-pity.
Help me to share and honestly reveal
    my secret problems.
O God, show me the way out.
Show me the way to make the worst known, for then
    I will honestly release my secret problems to those
    close to me and surrender them to You.
This suffering will pass.
This suffering I will use in understanding
    and helping others.

Fear

Dear God, fear used to be my worst enemy when I was locked up in my addiction. It prevented me from living fully. It kept me standing still. I now see how fear kept me a prisoner of my addiction and character defects. I will share my fears with You and others in the program. I pray to work to get past my fears.

Happy, Joyous, and Free

I am sure You want me to be
    happy, joyous, and free.
With Your help I will no longer believe
    that life has no meaning and is filled with sorrow.
You, the Twelve Steps, and our fellowship
    have shown me I made my own misery.
    You didn't do it.
I pray I will avoid the deliberate manufacture
    of misery.
But if trouble comes, I will cheerfully make it
    an opportunity to demonstrate Your wisdom
    and power.

It Shows in Your Face

You don't have to tell how you live each day;
You don't have to say if you work or play;
A tired, true barometer serves in the place.
However you live, it shows in your face.

The falseness, the deceit that you wear in your heart
Will not stay inside where it got its start;
For sinew and blood is a thin veil of lace.
However you live, it shows in your face.

If you have battled and won in the game of life,
If you feel you've conquered the sorrow and strife,
If you've played the game square and you stand
    on first base,
You don't have to tell it, it shows in your face.

If your life's been unselfish, for others you live,
And not what you get, but what you can give,
And you live close to God, in His infinite Grace,
You don't have to tell it, it shows in your face.

Happy Thoughts

Lord, remind me that the past is just that.
Protect me from my own thoughts.
Take away the old tapes playing in my head.
Fill my mind with thoughts of peace and serenity.
Lead me into the light, away from darkness.
Surround me with Your love.
God, remind me that yesterday is gone;
Tomorrow may never be;
Today is all I have.

Risk

To laugh is to risk appearing the fool.
To weep is to risk being called sentimental.
To reach out to another is to risk involvement.
To expose feelings is to risk showing your true self.
To place your ideas and dreams before the crowd
    is to risk being called naïve.
To love is to risk not being loved in return.
To live is to risk dying.
To hope is to risk despair.
To try is to risk failure.
But risks must be taken,
Because the greatest risk in life is to risk nothing.
The people who risk nothing do nothing,
Have nothing, are nothing, and become nothing.
They may avoid suffering and sorrow,
But they simply cannot learn to feel,
And change, and grow, and love, and live.
Chained by their servitude, they are slaves;
They have forfeited their freedom.
Only the people who risk are truly free.

Dwell in My Heart

O God, dwell in my heart,
Open it out, purify it, make it bright and beautiful,
Awaken it, prepare it, make it fearless,
Make it a blessing to others,
Rid it of laziness, free it from doubt,
Unite it with all, destroy its bondage,
Let Your peaceful music pervade all its works.
Make my heart useful to You and others.

Honesty, Purity, Unselfishness, and Love

Dear God, may I breathe in the inspiration
    of goodness and truth.
Breathe in the spirit of honesty, purity, unselfishness,
    and love.
They are readily available to me,
    if I am willing to accept them wholeheartedly.

God, You have given me two things:
    Your Spirit and the power of choice.
To accept or not,
    as I have the gift of free will.

When I choose the path of selfishness, greed, and
    pride, I am refusing to accept Your Spirit.
When I choose the path of love and service,
    I accept Your Spirit, and then it flows into me
    and makes all things new.

Daily Surrender—No Regrets

This I pray, Higher Power:

I will surrender to Your will today, which brings me peace and joy that makes all things new. I no longer have that trampled look of someone forced to remember every mistake he or she has made. I no longer hide under that blanket of regrets. My daily surrender to You and the fellowship that surrounds me leads me away from darkness and into the wonderful light of Your wisdom.

Surround Me with Your Light

Surround me with Your light;
Penetrate the very depths of my being with that light;
Let there remain no areas of darkness within me;
Clear away the shadows of my ego,
    the clouds of my defects;
Transform my whole being with the healing light of
    Your love;
Open me completely to receive your love,
    and help me to let go of all that blocks Your healing.

Search for Serenity

The search is yours and mine. Each finds his way with help, but yet alone.

Serenity is the goal. It comes to those who learn to wait and grow, for each can learn to understand himself and say, "I've found a joy in being me and knowing you, a knowledge of the depths I can descend, a chance to climb the heights above my head."

The way is not so easy all the time. Our feet will stumble often as we go. A friend may need to give some extra help, as we once gave to others when in the hour of fear.

This is no picnic path that we have found, but yet compared to other days and other times, it seems a better route.

We lost our way before, in fear, guilt, and resentments held too long. Self-pity had its way with us; we found the perfect alibi for all our faults.

We do not know what life may bring from day to day. Tomorrow is a task not yet begun, and we could fail to pass its test.

But this will wait, while in today we do the best we can. Today we try to grow. Today we live, we seek to know, to give, to share, with you.

To Change

I pray that I may continue to change, and I appreciate You for investing in me Your time, Your patience, Your understanding, and for seeing in me someone worthwhile. I am sorry for the past—but I will change for the better, and I am grateful for the opportunity.

Teach Me

Teach me, God, so that I might know
The way to change and the way to grow.
Give me the words to ask You how
To handle the here and live in the now.
Tempt me not with the valleys of death,
Give me freedom from fear in every breath.
And though mistakes I make in my daily life,
Deliver me from aiding strife.
Understand me, God, as I am now
And show me the furrows I need to plow
To reach my goal as a ripening food,
So I might feed others all that is good.
Fill me with energy known as the Power,
Until I come to rest at the midnight hour.

No Fear

I am a child of God
In God I live and move and have my being
So I have no fear
I am surrounded by the peace of God
And all is well
I am not afraid of people—
I am not afraid of things—
I am not afraid of circumstances—
I am not afraid of sickness
For God is with me
The peace of God fills my soul
And I have no fear.

Free from Fear

O God, for another day, for another morning, for another hour, for another chance to live and serve You, I am truly grateful. According to Your will, this day free me:

From fear of the future,
From anxiety of the morrow,
From bitterness toward anyone,
From cowardice in face of danger,
From laziness in face of work,
From failure before opportunity,
From weakness when Your power is at hand

And fill me with:

Love that knows no barrier,
Courage that cannot be shaken,
Faith through the darkness,
Strength sufficient for my tasks,
Loyalty to the fellowship,
Wisdom to meet life's complexities.

Be with me another day and use me as You will.

The Beatitudes

Blessed are the poor in spirit, for theirs is the kingdom
of heaven.
Blessed are they who mourn, for they shall
be comforted.
Blessed are the meek, for they shall inherit the earth.
Blessed are they who hunger and thirst after righteous-
ness, for they shall be filled.
Blessed are the merciful, for they shall obtain mercy.
Blessed are the pure in heart, for they shall see God.
Blessed are the peacemakers, for they shall be called
the children of God.
Blessed are they who are persecuted for righteous-
ness's sake, for theirs is the kingdom of heaven.

Becoming Whole

Dear God, I pray my physical, emotional, intellectual, and spiritual selves become one, a whole person again. I thank You for showing me how to match my outside to my inside. To laugh when I feel like laughing. To cry when I feel sad. To recognize my own anger or fear or guilt. I pray for wholeness.

To Grow and Blossom

Lord, I mourn the loss of my innocence. By sharing my experiences, I hope to recapture it. Lord, I long to feel more, trust more, laugh more, and live life fully. Show me the way, God. I thank You for my renewed sanity and my sobriety. When I have both, I can grow and blossom. Everyone in my family, the fellowship, and my neighborhood can benefit from my peace.

The Lord's Prayer

Our Father, Who art in heaven, hallowed be Thy Name. Thy kingdom come. Thy will be done, on earth as it is in heaven. Give us this day our daily bread. And forgive us our trespasses, as we forgive those who trespass against us. And lead us not into temptation, but deliver us from evil. For Thine is the kingdom and the power and the glory, forever and ever. Amen.

STEP SIX

❋

Willingness

SELF-ACCEPTANCE

•

VALUES: IN WITH THE NEW

•

ENTIRELY READY

These defects were never helpful:
They will not protect or save us.
Only a Higher Power and a willingness to change will.

Sixth Step Prayer

Dear God,
I am ready for Your help in removing from me the defects of character that I now realize are obstacles to my recovery. Help me to continue being honest with myself and guide me toward spiritual and mental health.

Set Aside Prayer

Lord, today help me set aside
    everything I think I know about You
Everything I think I know
    about myself
Everything I think I know
    about others and
Everything I think I know
    about my own recovery
For a new experience in myself
A new experience in my fellows
    and my own recovery.

Put Courage into My Heart

Lord, put courage into my heart,
   and take away what blocks me from Your will.
Free my speech so I may pass on Your goodness,
   so all will understand me.
Give me friends to advise and help me,
   that our efforts together may help others.
And, above all, let me constantly remember
   that my actions are useless if not guided
   by Your wisdom.

The Acceptance Prayer

God, grant me the serenity to accept my addiction gracefully and humbly. Grant me also the ability to absorb the teachings of the program, which by its past experience is trying to help me. Teach me to be grateful for the help I receive.

Guide me, Higher Power, in the path of tolerance and understanding of my fellow members and all humankind, guide me away from the path of criticism, intolerance, jealousy, and envy of my friends. Let me not prejudge; let me not become a moralist; keep my tongue and thoughts from malicious, idle gossip.

Help me to grow in stature spiritually, mentally, and morally. Grant me that greatest of all rewards, that of being able to help my fellow sufferers in their search out of the addiction that has encompassed them.

Above all, help me to be less critical and impatient with myself.

To Be Prayer

O Lord, I ain't what I ought to be,
And I ain't what I want to be,
And I ain't what I'm going to be,
But O Lord, I thank You
That I ain't what I used to be.

I Wish I Were

I wish I were big enough to honestly admit all my
    shortcomings,
Brilliant enough to accept praise without it making
    me arrogant,
Tall enough to tower over dishonesty,
Strong enough to welcome criticism,
Compassionate enough to understand human frailties,
Wise enough to recognize mistakes,
Humble enough to appreciate greatness,
Brave enough to stand by my friends,
Human enough to be thoughtful of my neighbor,
And spiritual enough to be devoted to the love of God.

I Am Me

In all of the world, there is no one else exactly like me. Everything that comes out of me is authentically mine because I alone choose it. I own everything about me: my body, my feelings, my mouth, my voice, all my actions, whether they be to others or to myself. I own my fantasies, my dreams, my hopes, my fears. I own all of my triumphs and successes, all of my failures and mistakes.

Because I own all of me, I can become intimately acquainted with me. By doing so, I can love me and be friendly with me in all of my parts. I know there are aspects about myself that puzzle me, and other aspects that I do not know, but as long as I am friendly and loving to myself, I can courageously look for solutions to the puzzles and for ways to find out more about me.

However I look and sound, whatever I say and do, and whatever I think and feel at a given moment in time is authentically me. If later some parts of how I looked, sounded, thought, and felt turn out to be unfitting, I can discard that which is unfitting, keep the rest, and invent something new for that which I discarded. I can see, hear, feel, think, say, and do. I have the tools to survive, to be close to others, to be productive, and to make sense and order out of the world of people and things outside of me, and therefore I can engineer me. I am me and I am okay.

As I Think

Higher Power, today with Your help, I'll remember:

As I think, I travel; and as I love, I attract. I am today where my thoughts have brought me; I will be tomorrow where my thoughts take me. I cannot escape the result of my thoughts, but I can endure and learn; I can accept and be glad. I will realize the vision (not the idle wish) of my heart, be it base or beautiful or a mixture of both, for I will always gravitate toward that which I, secretly, most love. Into my hands will be placed the exact result of my thoughts; I will receive that which I earn, no more, no less. Whatever my present environment may be, I will fall, remain, or rise with my thoughts, my vision, my attitudes. I will become as small as my controlling desire, as great as my dominant aspiration.

Your Destiny

Watch your thoughts;
    they become your words.
Watch your words;
    they become your actions.
Watch your actions;
    they become your habits.
Watch your habits;
    they become your character.
Watch your character;
    it becomes your destiny.

Where There Is Charity and Wisdom

Where there is charity and wisdom, there is neither fear nor ignorance.

Where there is patience and humility, there is neither anger nor annoyance.

Where there is love and joy, there is neither greed nor selfishness.

Where there is peace and meditation, there is neither anxiety nor doubt.

Self-Respect Prayer

O God, teach me that self-respect cannot be hunted. It cannot be purchased. It is never for sale. It comes to me when I am alone, in quiet moments, in quiet places, when I suddenly realize that, knowing the good, I have done it; knowing the beautiful, I have served it; knowing the truth, I have spoken it.

Unselfishness Prayer

Higher Power, guide me as I walk the narrow way between being selfish and unselfish. I know I must be selfish, to concentrate on my own recovery, so I do not slip and be of no use to myself or anyone else. Yet I must also be unselfish, reaching out to others, sensitive to their needs, and willing to meet them at any time. With Your help, I can do both, and keep a balance that will give me a proper perspective in my life.

Usefulness Prayer

God, help me today to find balance
Between my character defects and the
Principles of our program
So as to be useful
To myself, all others, and You,
The God of my understanding.

Unselfishness

Dear Lord,
I must continually work toward unselfishness.
To be unselfish is to be useful.
When I am selfish, I am useless to myself, You,
    and others.
Help me to stop thinking of only me
    and to stop hoarding not only material things
    but also my thoughts and feelings from others.

Dear Lord, grant that I may practice
    what the program teaches me.
My life has been saved by
    what others have given me.
I must, in turn, give it away to keep it.

Expectations

Higher Power, help me stop expecting so much from myself. I set unrealistic standards, and when they are not met, unhappiness follows. Help me be true to myself and only expect what I am capable of doing. As I grow in recovery and do my assignments every day, I am able to do more. Your will provides realistic goals. Your will provides what I need to succeed.

Knowledge

God, may I not fear new ideas and the wisdom offered to me in my recovery. Help me keep my mind open to hear the help that is offered and leave judgment to You. I'm able to hear more clearly when I work the Steps and let You work in my life. May I keep growing and accepting the knowledge that comes my way. When I don't know something, I will admit it. Knowing that I don't know is also knowledge.

Trust

Higher Power, when I was using, I trusted no one. I lied about everything. Cheating was a way of life. The only thing I could trust was my addiction. When I discovered that was the biggest lie of all, that was the greatest day of my life. Thank You, God, for helping me put my trust in the program, the Steps, my sponsor, my group, and You, my Higher Power. Little by little, day by day, I am learning to trust again. And the greatest blessing is that others are learning to trust me.

Be Patient with Everyone

Be patient with everyone, but above all with yourself . . .
do not be disappointed by your imperfections, but always
rise up with fresh courage. How are you to be patient in
dealing with your neighbor's faults if you are impatient
in dealing with your own? They who are worried by their
own shortcomings will not correct them. All positive
progress comes from a calm and peaceful mind.

A Prayer for Tolerance

Higher Power, help me to know the most lovable quality I can possess is tolerance. It is the vision that enables me to see things from another's viewpoint. It is the generosity that concedes to others the right to their own opinions and their own peculiarities. It is the bigness that enables me to let people be happy in their own way instead of my way.

Willingness and Action

God, help me remember that willingness without action is fantasy. I have left my fantasy life behind with my active addiction. The best way to get ready for action is to pray. Prayer makes me ready for success. Sometimes my prayers tell me to go right or left. Sometimes they just tell me to stand and wait for instructions. When I am willing to pray, I am willing to act. When I am willing, I am filled with prayer. Prayer always comes before action.

Power of Choice

Dear God, I pray for Your help
    in making the right choices.
I am, at any given moment of my life in recovery,
    the sum total of the choices I make.
I pray for Your guidance in choosing between
    positive and negative,
    humility and arrogance,
    gratitude and self-centeredness;
And if at times my choices prove wrong,
    help me to learn from those experiences.

In Fellowship

Whatever is true, whatever is noble,
Whatever is right, whatever is pure, whatever is lovely,
Whatever is unselfish—if anything is useful
    or praiseworthy—
I will think about such things.
The things I have learned and received and heard
    and seen in
Our fellowship and program, I will practice,
    and the God of
My understanding will be with me.

The Gratitude Prayer

O God, I want to thank You for bringing me this far
    along the road to recovery.
It is good to be able to get my feet on the floor again.
It is good to be able to do at least some things for
    myself again.
Best of all is to have the joy of feeling well again.
O God, keep me grateful,
Grateful to all of the people who helped me back to
    health,
Grateful to You for the way in which You have brought
    me through it all.
O God, give me patience.
Help me to not be in too big a hurry to do too much.
Help me to keep on doing what I'm told to do.
Help me to be so obedient to those who know what is
    best for me that very soon I shall be on the top of
    the world and on the top of my job again.
I can say what the psalmist said:
"I waited patiently for the Lord;
He inclined to me and heard my cry.
He took me from a fearful pit, and from the miry clay,
And on a rock He set my feet, establishing my way."

Let Go Completely

Do everything with a mind that lets go.
Do not expect any praise or reward.
If you let go a little, you will have a little peace.
If you let go a lot, you will have a lot of peace.
If you let go completely, you will know complete peace
    and freedom.
Your struggles with the world
Will have come to an end.

STEP SEVEN

❉

Humility and Surrender

OUR LIMITATIONS

·

HUMBLE GROWTH

·

RELIEF

·

THE CALM AFTER

With the help of our Higher Power,
We can choose goodness,
And we do.

Seventh Step Prayer

My Creator, I am now willing that You should have all of me, good and bad. I pray that You now remove from me every single defect of character which stands in the way of my usefulness to You and my fellows. Grant me strength, as I go out from here, to do Your bidding. Amen.

Prayer for Healing

Higher Power,

You have told us to ask and we will receive, to seek and we will find, to knock and You will open the door to us.

I trust in Your love for me and in the healing power of Your compassion. I praise You and thank You for the mercy You have shown to me.

Higher Power, I am sorry for all my mistakes. I ask for Your help in removing the negative patterns of my life. I accept with all my heart Your forgiving love.

I ask for the grace to be aware of the character defects that exist within myself. Let me not offend You by my weak human nature, or by my impatience, resentment, or neglect of people who are a part of my life. Rather, teach me the gift of understanding and the ability to forgive, just as You continue to forgive me.

I seek Your strength and Your peace so that I may become Your instrument in sharing those gifts with others.

Guide me in my prayer that I might know what needs to be healed and how to ask You for that healing.

It is You, Higher Power, whom I seek. Please enter the door of my heart and fill me with the presence of Your spirit now and forever.

I thank You, God, for doing this.

Facing Indecision

Dear God, help me during the day when I face indecision. Help me when I do not know which course to take. I ask You for inspiration, an intuitive thought, or a decision. You have instructed me during these times of indecision not to struggle, to relax and take it easy. You will provide the right answers. This I pray.

O Great Spirit

O Great Spirit,

Whose voice I hear in the winds, and whose breath gives life to all the world, hear me! I am small and weak, I need Your strength and wisdom. Let me walk in beauty, and make my eyes ever behold the red and purple sunset.

Make my hands respect the things You have made, and my ears sharp to hear Your voice.

Make me wise so that I may understand the things You have taught my people.

Let me learn the lessons You have hidden in every leaf and rock.

I seek strength, not to be greater than my brother, but to fight my greatest enemy: myself.

Make me always ready to come to You with clean hands and straight eyes.

So when life fades, as the fading sunset, my spirit may come to You without shame.

Easy Does It

Dear God, help me remember to take things slowly, for spiritual progress requires time for growth. Maturity is not an overnight miracle. Help me to be productive and keep me from procrastinating or being impatient and rushing ahead too quickly. I will remind myself today not to push myself faster than I need to go. I won't push the river; I'll let it flow.

Blessing from Lao Tzu

Follow diligently the Way in your own heart,
    but make no display of it to the world.
Keep behind, and you shall be put in front.
Keep out, and you shall be kept in.
He who humbles himself shall be preserved entire.
He who bends shall be made straight.
He who is empty shall be filled.
He who is worn out shall be renewed.

Humility

Humility is perpetual quietness of heart. It is to have no trouble. It is never to be worried or angered, irritable or distressed, to wonder at nothing that is done to me, to feel nothing done against me. It is to be at rest when nobody praises me, and when I am blamed or despised; it is to have a blessed home in myself where I can go in and shut the door and kneel to my Father in secret and be at peace, as in a deep sea of calmness, when all around and about seems troubled.

The Gift of Humility

Grant upon us, O God, the gift of humility. When we speak, teach us to give our opinion quietly and sincerely. When we do well in work or play, give us a sense of proportion, that we be neither unduly elated nor foolishly self-deprecatory. Help us in success to realize what we owe to You and the efforts of others; in failure, to avoid self-pity; and in all ways to be simple and natural, quiet in manner, and reasonable in thought.

The Strength of Humility

Higher Power, I have learned in recovery that there is no greater defense against the cunning, baffling, and powerful disease than a humble attitude. I pray for understanding that there is strength and wisdom that come from true humility. Humility has nothing to do with shyness, weakness, or putting myself down. Humility is living in a proper relationship with You. When I walk with You, I don't have to try to be humble. I am humble.

Shinto Blessing

I humbly speak in the presence of the Great Parent God:
I pray that this day, the whole day, as a child of God,
I may not be taken hold of by my own desire but demonstrate the Divine Glory by living a life of creativeness,
which shows forth the true individual.

My Daily Prayer

God, I turn my will and my life over to You this day for Your keeping. Your will, Lord, not mine. I ask for Your guidance and direction. I will walk humbly with You and all humankind. You are giving me a grateful heart for my many blessings. You are removing the defects of character that stand in my way. You are giving me freedom from self-will.

Let love, compassion, and understanding be in my every thought, word, and deed this day. I release to You those who have mistreated me. I truly desire Your abundance of truth, love, harmony, and peace. As I go out today to do Your bidding, let me help anyone I can who is less fortunate than I.

Empty Out

O God, thank You for my spiritual growth and especially that gradual walk into Your light, which has seemed to be a process of breaking down—of disorganization, of emptying out—a matter of deflation in my own self-importance until self-approval and concern for the approval of others has shrunk to a point where I'm willing to step entirely aside and give You a chance to shine.

The Grace of God

God's grace is a gift. Grace is the love and generosity of God. Not until we felt defeated and made an active surrender were we open to this gift of help from our Higher Power.

I pray to receive God's grace in its many forms. It is the hope we feel after a good night's rest, the good feelings we get attending our meetings. I pray to stop trying to control everything and to stop missing the many gifts of God's grace. The grace of God surrounds me even in difficult times. Returning to that message renews my strength.

What I Ought to Know

Grant me, O Lord, to know what I ought to know,
    to love what I ought to love,
    to praise what pleases You most,
    to value what is important in Your eyes.
Do not allow me to judge others according
    to the sight of my eyes only,
    or to pass judgment according to gossip,
    but to know what is true and spiritual,
    and above all to always pray for what
    is good according to Your will.

Peace in Our Hearts

Our Creator, show us the way of patience, tolerance,
And kindness. Grant us power in our love,
Strength in our humility,
Clarity in our thinking,
Purity in our zeal,
Sincerity in our purpose,
Kindness in our laughter,
Value in our gratitude,
Compassion in our friendships,
And Your peace in our hearts at all times.

Make Me

God, who touches earth with beauty,
Make me lovely too;
With Your Spirit re-create me,
Make my heart anew.

Like Your springs and running waters,
Make me crystal pure;
Like Your rocks of towering grandeur,
Make me strong and sure.

Like Your dancing waves in sunlight,
Make me glad and free;
Like the straightness of the pine trees,
Let me upright be.

Like the arching of the heavens,
Lift my thoughts above;
Turn my dreams to noble action,
Ministries of love.

God, who touches earth with beauty,
Make me lovely too;
Keep me ever, by Your Spirit,
Pure and strong and true.

Teach Me Your Will

Lord, take me from insanity;
Show me the way to serenity;
Remove my shortcomings;
Guide me toward forgiveness;
Remind me of my will;
Teach me Your will.
God, I ask that You love me
    until I am able to love myself;
Believe in me as I learn to believe in You;
Trust me until I can trust completely in You;
Be with me now just as You have been
    with me in the past.

True Power

Take from me, Higher Power, my false pride and grandiosity, all my phoniness and self-importance, and help me find the courage that shows itself in gentleness, the wisdom that shows itself in simplicity, and the true power that shows itself in modesty and humility.

Release Me

Lord, keep me from the habit of thinking I must say something on every subject and on every occasion.

Release me from wanting to control everyone's affairs.

Keep my mind free from the recital of endless details—give me wings to get to the point.

I ask for grace enough to listen to the tales of others' pains. Help me to endure them with patience, but seal my lips on my own aches and pains—they are increasing and my love of rehearsing them is becoming sweeter as the years go by.

Teach me the glorious lesson that occasionally it is possible that I may be mistaken.

Keep me reasonably sweet. I do not want to be a saint—some of them are so difficult to live with—but a sour old person is one of the crowning works of the devil.

Give me the ability to see good things in unexpected places, and talents in unexpected people. And give me, O Lord, the grace to tell them so.

Make me thoughtful, but not moody; helpful, but not bossy. With my vast store of wisdom, it seems a pity to not use it all, but you know, Lord, that I want a few friends at the end.

Our Possessions

Father of Light, teach us to value our possessions
    in the right way.
Help us never to think more of them than of people.
Make us ready to use them freely for the good of
    others
And to share them generously without complaining.
Thank You for the beautiful things we enjoy
    possessing.
May our enjoyment be wholesome and right and may
    we hold to all we own.

Earth Teach Me to Remember

Earth teach me stillness
    as the grasses are stilled with light.
Earth teach me suffering
    as old stones suffer with memory.
Earth teach me humility
    as blossoms are humble with beginning.
Earth teach me caring
    as the mother who secures her young.
Earth teach me courage
    as the tree which stands alone.
Earth teach me limitation
    as the ant which crawls on the ground.
Earth teach me freedom
    as the eagle which soars in the sky.
Earth teach me resignation
    as the leaves which die in the fall.
Earth teach me regeneration
    as the seed which rises in the spring.
Earth teach me to forget myself
    as melted snow forgets its life.
Earth teach me to remember kindness
    as dry fields weep in the rain.

God's Answer

I asked You, God, for strength that I might achieve;
I was made weak that I might learn humbly to obey.
I asked for help that I might do greater things;
I was given infirmity that I might do better things.
I asked for riches that I might be happy;
I was given poverty that I might be wise.
I asked for power that I might have the praise of men;
I was given weakness that I might feel the need for You.
I asked for all things that I might enjoy life;
I was given life that I might enjoy all things.
No, dear Lord, I've gotten nothing that I asked for
But everything I had hoped for.
Despite myself, my prayers were answered,
And I am among those most richly blessed.

So My Heart Is Quiet

Lord, I have given up my pride
    and turned away from my arrogance.
I am not concerned with great matters
    or with subjects too difficult for me.
Instead, I am content and at peace.
As a child lies quietly in its mother's arms,
    so my heart is quiet within me.

Thank You, God

Thank You, God, for all You have given me.
Thank You for all You have taken from me.
But, most of all, I thank You, God,
    for what You've left me:
Recovery, along with peace of mind, faith,
    hope, and love.

Thanks Again, God

Thank You, God, for hearing my prayers and granting
    my requests.
Thank You for the kindness You have shown me and
    the good people who surround me.
Thank You for giving me this new life in recovery
    and your great patience in helping me
    with my shortcomings.
Thank You for protecting me from the things that
    tempt me, and may my thoughts and actions
    demonstrate my gratitude to You.

All Actions Are Born in Thought

I now journey in the realm of the Spirit;
Your wisdom has helped me be willing to change,
Your love has helped me believe I can change,
Your grace has helped me make the right decisions,
Your power has helped me take the right actions.
Today, this I believe:
All negative actions are born in negative thought.
All positive actions are born in positive thought.
Help me always to know this is true.

Serene Days

God of the seas, to You I pray:
Bless unto me these serene days.

From these wide seas give unto me
A larger heart of charity.

May these strong tides wash out my mind
From all that's bitter and unkind.

With the broad beat of seabird's wings
Lift up my soul to heavenly things.

By the far sight of hills untrod
Call me to undared ventures, God.

Grant that these serene days may be
Your holy days indeed to me.

STEP EIGHT

❖

Reflection and Responsibility

A DEFECT'S MARK
·
ATONEMENT'S PRECURSOR

Our defects were not without victims.
We told ourselves that we hurt only ourselves,
But we hurt many.
Even one is too many.

Eighth Step Prayer

Higher Power, I ask Your help in making my list of all those I have harmed. I will take responsibility for my mistakes and be forgiving to others just as You are forgiving to me. Grant me the willingness to begin my restitution. This I pray.

Resent Somebody

The moment you start to resent a person, you become that person's slave. He or she controls your dreams, absorbs your digestion, robs you of your peace of mind and goodwill, and takes away the pleasure of your work.

A person you resent ruins your spirituality and nullifies your prayers. You cannot take a vacation without that person going along! He or she destroys your freedom of mind and hounds you wherever you go. There is no way to escape the person you resent.

That person is with you when you are awake and invades your privacy when you sleep. That person is close beside you when you eat, when you drive your car, and when you are on the job.

You can never have efficiency or happiness. The person you resent influences even the tone of your voice. He or she requires you to take medicine for indigestion, headaches, and loss of energy. That person even steals your last moment of consciousness before you go to sleep.

So if you want to be a slave, harbor your resentments.

Free of Resentment Prayer

God, free me from my resentment
Toward _____.
Please bless _____ in whatever it is that You know
They may be needing this day.
Please give _____ everything I want for myself.
And may _____ life be full of health, peace,
Prosperity, and happiness as they seek to have
A closer relationship with You.

Forgiving Others

Dear Lord, if I am unable or unwilling to forgive others for their actions, I will be unable to forgive myself for my actions. The agony of resentment, guilt, remorse, and shame will overpower me. These emotions will halt my progress toward the comfortable and rewarding living we are promised in working our recovery program.

Dear Lord, help me to pray for those who anger me and make me uncomfortable, and those whom I think have wronged me. You have instructed me that forgiveness will always triumph over guilt and shame. Remind me that my recovery is one-third love and two-thirds forgiveness.

Living Right

Higher Power, deliver me
  From the cowardice that dare not face new truth;
  From the laziness that is contented with half-truth;
  From the arrogance that thinks it knows all truth.
These things, good Lord, that I pray for,
Give me the strength to work for.

All That We Ought

All that we ought to have thought and have not
    thought,
All that we ought to have said and have not said,
All that we ought to have done and have not done;
All that we ought not to have thought and yet have
    thought,
All that we ought not to have spoken and yet have
    spoken,
All that we ought not to have done and yet have done;
For thoughts, words, and works, pray we, O God, for
    forgiveness,
And repent with penance.

Patience for My Family

God, give me patience for my family members,
For their criticism and unkind words,
For their loud outbursts and often drunken ways.
Remind me of their kind words and support,
Their sober moments of tenderness and love.
Allow me to find the good that each of them possesses.
They are my family, and I love them unconditionally.

My Chosen Life

Dear God, help me live the life I have chosen and allow others to do the same. It's hard to live more than one life at a time. Keep me free from trying to organize everyone's life according to my plan. Help me turn over my self-assumed responsibility for other people's lives to You. "Live and let live" is the Twelve Step way of life.

The Tolerance Prayer

Lord, give me tolerance toward those whose thoughts and ways, in the program and life, conflict with mine. For though I would, I cannot always know what constitutes the Absolute Truth. The other person may be right, while I may be all wrong, yet unaware.

Lord, make my motives right, for only this can ease my conscience when I sometimes err.

Lord, give me tolerance, for who am I to stand in judgment of another person's mistakes? No one knows better than my inward self how many little blunders I have and can make.

Life is full of stones that somehow trip us, and meaning not, we stumble now and then.

Lord, give me tolerance, for only You are rightly fit to judge my fellow travelers.

Always Remember

There is no growth without pain (pain is not optional), so hurt a little bit.

There is no laughter without tears, so cry often. (Don't be ashamed to cry, for if you don't, you will be ever secure but always lonely.)

There is no peace without first knowing turmoil in the soul, so be at war with yourself sometimes.

There is no grace without first wrestling with guilt. If you are wrestling, let God's grace surround you and give you new life.

Lord, I'm Hurting

Yes, Lord, I hurt.
The pain is deep,
And I feel the mountains
Are so steep.
I cannot seem to stand.
Please, dear Lord,
Take my hand.
I cannot seem to find my way.
For me the sun
Is not shining today.
I know You're there;
I've felt Your presence near,
But now, my Lord,
My heart is gripped with fear.
Lord, help the sun to shine
And to know
That You are mine.
Heal this pain I feel;
Make Your presence very real.
Today, Lord, I give You all.
Hold me tight,
So I can feel
Your strength and might.

I Cannot Do This Alone

O God, help me pray and concentrate my thoughts
on You:
    I cannot do this alone.
    In me there is darkness,
    But with You there is light;
    I am lonely, but You do not leave me;
    I am feeble in heart, but with You there is help;
    I am restless, but with You there is patience;
    I do not understand Your ways,
    But You know the way for me.

God Is Our Shelter

God is our shelter and strength,
    always ready to help in times of trouble.
So we will not be afraid, even if the earth is shaken . . .
    even if the seas roar and rage,
    and the hills are shaken by violence.
The Lord Almighty is with us.

Happy Days

My Creator, take me back to my childhood,
When I was carefree and innocent,
When my heart was filled with laughter and love,
When joy surrounded me,
When I had no responsibilities, no concerns.
I give thanks for those memories;
I cling to them.

For when my life is spinning out of control,
It may seem that way for only a moment,
Sometimes for a day, perhaps an entire week.

Thank You, God, for the memories of childhood.
I remember them; I feel relaxed and relieved.
I remember I've known peace and joy before.
When all is spinning out of control,
I will know peace and joy again.

Please, Lord

Please, Lord, teach us to laugh again;
but God, don't ever let us forget that we cried.

Moment by Moment

Never a trial
    God is not there.
Never a burden that
    God does not bear.
Never a sorrow that
    God does not share.
Moment by moment
    I'm under God's care.

Let Nothing Disturb Me

Let nothing disturb me,
Nothing frighten me.
All things are passing;
Patient endurance
Attains all things;
Whoever has God lacks nothing.
If I only have God,
I have more than enough.

I've Found a Reason

Dear God, as long as my life was preoccupied with my own problems, my own unwillingness and dark moods, I was critical, insensitive, rigid, and defiant. But when I honestly faced my defects and failures, and the worst was known and surrendered to You, the whole nature of living changed. I am no longer the emotional center of all things, and I no longer take everything as personal to myself. I've found a reason for all the suffering through which I have passed. It is to be used in understanding and helping others. Out of darkness comes light.

Awareness, Acceptance, Action

Dear God, slow me down when all I do is try to fix and control things and people. Help me to first accept situations as they are when I become aware of them. Slow me down in Your stillness. Mark my awareness with unselfishness, my acceptance with humility, and my actions with usefulness to me and others.

Gratitude and Joy

Dear God,

May I write the wrongs done to me in sand, but write the good things that happen to me in stone. Help me let go of all emotions such as resentment and retaliation, which diminish me, and hold on to the emotions such as gratitude and joy, which increase me.

Mend Me

Lord, help me to right my wrongs.
There are so many years of pain and heartache.
I seek the words that will help to heal the hearts
    of those I have broken—there are many.
I must mend them without further damaging them.
Some heal with each day I remain clean and sober.
Others will take more time.
Guide me and grant me patience and sympathy
    for the ones I have hurt and want only to love.

STEP NINE

✼

Love and Restitution

ACCOUNTABILITY

·

ATONEMENT

·

LOVE AND RESTITUTION

We act again in pure grace:
Forgiveness embodied,
We return to others, we atone,
And we love.

Ninth Step Prayer

Higher Power, I pray for the right attitude to make my amends, being ever mindful not to harm others in the process. I ask for Your guidance in making indirect amends. Most important, I will continue to make amends by staying abstinent, helping others, and growing in spiritual progress.

That Great Purpose

Keep making progress in your Twelve Step recovery.
Let your aim be as steady as a star.
Let the world battle and stress.
You may be assaulted, hassled,
　　insulted, slandered, wounded, and rejected.
You may be chased by enemies,
　　abused by them, forgotten by friends,
　　hated and rejected by others,
　　but see to it
　　that with steady determination
　　and with unfaltering devotion,
　　you pursue that great purpose of your life
　　and the object of your being
　　until at last you can say:
　　"I have finished the work that You,
　　dear God, have given me to do."

Self-Seeking Slips Away

Today, God, help me remember not everything is about me. When I was using, thinking of myself was my whole existence. With abstinence, I began to practice understanding, humility, gratitude, caring, and sharing with others. By having faith in our program's recovery Steps and their other-centered focus, I am reminded that I am a person who truly needs other people.

Reconstruction Ahead

My Creator, show me the way of patience, tolerance, kindness, and love. Help me to clean house and ask in my morning prayer and meditation for the energy for positive action. I have accepted the reality that there is a long period of reconstruction ahead. And yes, the spiritual life is not a theory; I have to live it.

No Greater Power

To find direction and meaning, I must tap a Higher Power. That Power is God as I understand Him. I will start each day with God and take Steps Three, Seven, and Eleven. There is no Greater Power. And then I say:

Lord, I turn my life and will over to You today.

I will walk humbly with You and my fellow travelers.

You are giving me a grateful heart for my many blessings.

You are directing my thinking and separating me from self-pity, dishonesty, and self-seeking motives.

You are removing my resentments, fears, and other character defects that stand in my way.

You are giving me freedom from self-will.

Your will, Lord, not mine.

You will show me today what I can do to help someone who is still hurting.

As I go out today to do Your bidding,

You are helping me to become a better person.

Changes

Today I pray that I may understand there are some things
I cannot change:

I cannot change the weather.
I cannot change the tick of the clock.
I cannot change the past.
I cannot change another person
   against his or her will.
I cannot change what is right and wrong.
I cannot change the fact that a relationship ended.

I can stop worrying over that which I cannot
   change and enjoy living more! I can place those
   things into the hands of my Higher Power.
   Save energy. Let go. Instead of trying to change
   someone else:
I can change my attitude.
I can change my list of priorities.
I can change my bad habits into good ones.
I can move from the place of brokenness
   into wholeness, in the beautiful person
   God created me to become.

Today's Thought

I am but one, but I am one;
I can't do everything,
But I can do *something;*
What I can do, I ought to do,
What I ought to do, God helping me,
I will do.

Amelia Earhart's Prayer

Courage is the price that life exacts
 for granting peace.
The soul that knows it not, knows no release
 from little things;
Knows not the livid loneliness of fear
 nor mountain heights,
 where bitter joy can hear
 the sound of wings.

Searcy W.'s Prayer

I pray today to:
    Trust God,
    Clean house,
    Help others.

Saving the World

Today may my prayers help me realize
I cannot control everything.
To put the world in order,
We must first put the nation in order;
To put the nation in order,
We must first put the family in order;
To put the family in order,
We must first cultivate our personal life;
We must first set our hearts right.

First Things First

Dear Higher Power, remind me:
    To tidy up my own mind,
    To keep my sense of values straight,
    To sort out the possible and the impossible,
    To turn the impossible over to You,
    And get busy on the possible.

Guide Me

Thank You, Higher Power, for this beautiful day,
   for strength, for health.
Help me to live this day for You.
Place in my path some way to serve others.
Help me to know that no other walks in my shoes,
   that there is something that only I can do today.
Guide my thoughts and deeds that I may feel
   Your presence today and in all the tomorrows.

Open Mind

Higher Power, may I understand:

To be alert to my own needs, not to the faults of others;
To remain teachable;
To listen;
To keep an open mind; and
To learn not who's right but what's right.

The Gorsedd Prayer

Grant us, O God, Your protection;
And in Your protection, strength;
And in strength, understanding;
And in understanding, knowledge;
And in knowledge, the knowledge of justice;
And in the knowledge of justice, the love of justice;
And in the love of justice, the love of existence;
And in the love of existence, the love of God,
God and all goodness.

The Great Reality

Let the Great Reality govern my every thought, and Truth be the heart of my life. For so it must be for all of humanity. Please help me to do "my part." And may the intensity of all our egos become the Joy of our One Soul.

I Ask Not for Easier Tasks

O God, I ask not for easier tasks.
I ask for stronger aptitudes and greater talents
    to meet any tasks which may come my way.
Help me to help others so their lives
    may be made easier and happier.
Strengthen my confidence in others
    in spite of what they may do or say.
Give me strength to live according to the Golden Rule,
    enthusiasm to inspire those around me,
        sympathy to help lighten the burdens of those
    who suffer, and a spirit of joy and gladness to share
    with others.

Release Hurt, Anger, Resentment

God of Reason, I am willing to release all feelings
    of hurt and anger and resentment.
Help me know true forgiveness
    and see each person as part of You.
Let my words and my actions
    serve only to honor You.
May my honest and positive action
    heal and comfort and harmonize my life
    and the lives of those around me.
Thank You, God.

May I Encourage Others

Dear Lord, may I remember to encourage others,
    truly listen to what others say,
    encourage their expression of ideas and feelings
    by exercising patience and empathy,
    rewarding honesty and openness with affirmation.
You have instructed us to encourage one another,
    build one another up,
    be at peace among ourselves,
    always seek to do good to one another,
    rejoice always,
    pray constantly,
    for this is Your will.

Comes the Dawn

After a while you learn the subtle difference between holding a hand and chaining a soul. And you learn that love doesn't mean leaning and company doesn't mean security. And you begin to learn that kisses aren't contracts, and presents aren't promises.

And you begin to accept your defeats with your head up and your eyes open, with the grace of a grown-up, not the grief of a child.

And you learn to build all your roads on today because tomorrow's ground is too uncertain for plans, and futures have a way of falling down in mid-flight.

After a while you learn that even sunshine burns if you get too much. So you plant your own garden and decorate your own soul, instead of waiting for someone to bring you flowers.

And you learn that you really can endure, that you really are strong, and you really do have worth.

And you learn and learn. . . . With every good-bye, you learn.

Heart of a Child

Grant me, O God,
The heart of a child,
Pure and transparent as a spring;
A simple heart,
Which never harbors sorrows;
A heart glorious in self-giving,
Tender in compassion;
A heart faithful and generous,
Which will never forget any good
Or bear a grudge for any evil.

Make me a heart gentle and humble,
Loving without asking in return,
Large-hearted and undauntable,
Which no ingratitude can sour,
And no indifference weary;
A heart born to help others,
Usefulness never measured.

Blessings by the Buddha

May every creature abound in well-being and peace.
May every living being, weak or strong, the long and
    the small, the short and the medium-sized, the
    mean and the great,
May every living being, seen and unseen, those living
    far off, those nearby, those already born, those
    waiting to be born,
May all attain inward peace.

Let no one deceive another,
Let no one despise another in any situation,
Let no one, from apathy or hatred, wish evil to anyone
    at all.
Just as a mother, with her own life, protects her child
    from hurt,
So within yourself foster a limitless concern for every
    living creature.

Display a heart of boundless love for all the world
In all its height and depth and broad extent,
Love unrestrained, without hate or hostility.
Then as you stand or walk, sit or lie, until overcome by
    drowsiness, devote your mind entirely to this;
It is known as living here life divine.

Speak Your Truth

Speak your truth.
Listen when others speak theirs too.
When you let go of fear, you will learn to love others
     and you will let them love you.
Do not be afraid of dying.
But do not be afraid to live.
Ask yourself what that means.
Open your heart to love, for that is why you're here.
And know that you are, and always have been,
     One with God and all who live.

Love

Higher Power, remind me that:

Love is patient;
Love is kind.
Love is not jealous; it does not put on airs; it is not
   snobbish.
Love is never rude; it is not self-seeking; it is not prone
   to anger; neither does it brood over injuries.
Love does not rejoice in what is wrong, but rejoices
   with the truth.
There is no limit to love's forbearance, its truth,
   its hope, its power to endure.

Love Is

Love is friendship that has caught fire. It is quiet understanding, mutual confidence, sharing, and forgiving. It is loyalty through good times and bad. It settles for less than perfection and makes allowances for human weaknesses.

Love is content with the present, it hopes for the future, and it doesn't brood over the past. It's the day-in-and-day-out chronicle of irritations, problems, compromises, small disappointments, big victories, and common goals.

If you have love in your life, it can make up for a great many things you lack. If you don't have it, no matter what else there is, it's not enough.

My Family

Help me accept the potent emotions I may feel toward family members. Help me be grateful for the lesson they are teaching me. I accept the golden light of healing that is now shining on me and my family. I thank God that healing does not always come in a neat, tidy package.

Lord, I Bring Before You

Lord, I bring before You
The needs of my parents, friends,
Brothers, sisters,
All whom I love,
And all who have asked me to pray for them.

I pray that they may experience Your help
And the gift of Your comfort,
Protection from all dangers,
Deliverance from all sin,
And freedom from pain.
May they give You joyful thanks and praise.

Lord, in Your mercy, forgive all our sins against
    one another.
Take from our hearts
All suspicion, hard feelings,
Anger, dissension,
And whatever else may diminish the love
We should have for one another.

We Are One

I am one with my father and the universe.
I am one with mother earth.
I am one with everyone within the reach of my voice.
And, in this togetherness, we ask the divine
    intelligence to eradicate all negatives from
    our hearts, from our minds, from our worlds,
    and from our actions.
And, so be it.

Thanksgiving Prayer

Great and Eternal Mystery of Life, Creator of All Things, I give thanks for the beauty You put in every single one of Your creations.

I am grateful that You did not fail in making every stone, plant, creature, and human being a perfect and whole part of the Sacred Hoop.

I am grateful that You have allowed me to see the strength and beauty of All My Relations.

My humble request is that all of the children of Earth will learn to see the same perfection themselves.

May none of Your human children doubt or question Your wisdom, grace, and sense of wholeness in giving all of Creation a right to be living extensions of Your perfect love.

Apache Blessing

Now you will feel no rain,
For each of you will be shelter for another.

Now you will feel no cold,
For each of you will be warmth to another.

Now there will be no loneliness,
For each of you will be companion to another.

Now you are separate persons,
But there is only one road before you.

May beauty surround you all
In journeys ahead and through all the years.

May happiness be your companion and
Your days together will be good and long
    upon the earth.

STEP TEN

❖

Growth and Vigilance

OUR MOMENT
·
OUR CODE
·
OUR GRACE

May we always remember,
The code, the grace, and the moment
To which we have promised ourselves
Forevermore.

Tenth Step Prayer

I pray I may continue:

To grow in understanding and effectiveness;
To take daily spot-check inventories of myself;
To correct mistakes when I make them;
To take responsibility for my actions;
To be ever aware of my negative and self-defeating
    attitudes and behaviors;
To keep my willfulness in check;
To always remember I need Your help;
To keep love and tolerance of others as my code;
And to continue to explore in daily prayer how I can
    best serve You, my Higher Power.

Living in the Present

One day at a time,
This is enough.
Do not look back and grieve over the past,
For it is gone . . .
And do not be troubled about the future,
For it has not yet come.
Live in the present, and make it so beautiful
That it will be worth remembering.

New Day

Thank You, God, for today.

This is the beginning of a new day. I can waste it or use it for good.

What I do today is important because I am exchanging a day of my life for it.

When tomorrow comes, this day will be gone forever—leaving in its place something I have traded for it.

I want it to be gain, not loss; good, not evil; success, not failure; in order that I shall not regret the price I paid for today.

Our True Home

Our true home is in the present moment.
To live in the present moment is a miracle.
The miracle is not to walk on water.
The miracle is to walk on the green earth
    in the present moment,
To appreciate the peace and beauty
    that are available now.
Peace is all around us—
In the world and in nature—
And within us—
In our bodies and our spirits.
Once we learn to touch this peace,
We will be healed and transformed.
It is not a matter of faith;
It is a matter of practice.

Sanskrit Proverb

Look to this day,
For it is life,
The very life of life.
In its brief course lies all
The realities and verities of existence,
The bliss of growth,
The splendor of action,
The glory of power.
For yesterday is but a dream,
And tomorrow is only a vision.
But today, well lived,
Makes every yesterday a dream of happiness
And every tomorrow a vision of hope.
Look well, therefore, to this day.

Recovery Prayer

Today and every day, I pray to be ever mindful that recovery is the most important thing in my life, without exception. I may believe my job, or my home life, or one of many other things comes first. But if I don't stay with the program, chances are I won't have a job, a family, sanity, or even life. If I am convinced that everything in life depends on my recovery, I have a much better chance of improving my life. If I put other things first, I am only hurting my chances.

Enough to Need

Dear God, never allow me to think that I have knowledge enough to need no teaching, wisdom enough to need no correction, talents enough to need no grace, goodness enough to need no progress, humility enough to need no repentance, devotion enough to need no improvement, strength sufficient without Thy Spirit, lest, standing still, I fall back forevermore.

The Four A's

Dear God, I have learned to live within my limitations and to live up to my capabilities as I grow in recovery. As I try to practice the principles of our program, I will accept the truth that I seek progress and not spiritual perfection. I pray to admit my limitations and remind myself I am only human. I have quit trying to play God. When I take my inventory and remember the Four A's—Acceptance, Awareness, Action, and Attitude—I continue learning to live within my limitations and to live up to my capabilities.

The Simple Things

Lord, I pray to stay uncomplicated and do well
these simple tasks:

    If I open it, I will close it.

    If I turn it on, I will turn it off.

    If I unlock it, I will lock it up.

    If I break it, I will admit it.

    If I borrow it, I will return it.

    If I make a mess, I will clean it up.

    If I value it, I will take care of it.

    If it will brighten someone's day, I will say it!

May My Thoughts Be Guided

Dear Lord, You have guided me to demonstrate
    that common sense is the best approach
    to living in this recovery program.

The Tenth Step suggests it is wise to
    pause often and review all my choices.
My hurried remarks and actions lead to mistakes.
I have learned when I am wrong to promptly admit it.

From this I have learned
    honesty and humility.
From this I have grown
    in understanding and effectiveness.

Dear Lord, in gratitude I pray:
I am what I think.
All that I am comes from my thoughts.
With my thoughts and positive actions,
    I make my world.

Quiet My Mind

Dear Lord, teach me to quiet my mind.
Stop my thoughts from racing from one thing
    to another.
Stop me from the obsessive thinking about the lives
    of others.
Help me rest and quiet my mind.
Help me let go of trying to control the lives of others.
Free my mind to be at rest.
This I pray.

Honest and Sincere

Dear God,
Help me to realize this day that it is Your will,
Not mine that is to be done, and then to do it.

Help me to accept myself as I am,
But to constantly hope that I may become better.

Help me to forgive, to love, and to accept others
But to ask for absolutely nothing in return.

Help me to be grateful for what I have and to accept
More only if You will it.

Help me to receive tenderness as well as to give it.

Help me to be honest and sincere with myself,
But to remember with a smile how little I am.

Help me, above all, to have utter faith in You as
My friend and leader.

Help me to re-create the mood of this prayer
Every twenty-four hours.

Do It Now

Dear God,

I expect to pass through this world but once.

Any good thing, therefore, that I can do, or any kindness I can show to any fellow traveler, let me do it now.

Let me not defer nor neglect it, for I shall not pass this way again.

All the Good I Can

Dear God, guide me to
Do all the good I can
By all means I can
In all ways I can
In all places I can
To all people I can
As long as I can.

Continue to Watch

I have entered the world of the Spirit;
I will grow in understanding and effectiveness;
I will continue to watch for
    selfishness, dishonesty, resentment, and fear.
When these crop up,
    I will ask You at once to remove them.
I will discuss these defects with someone immediately
    and make amends quickly if I have harmed anyone.
Then I will resolutely turn my thoughts
    to someone I can help.
Love and tolerance of others is my code.

Kindness Prayer

Keep us, O God, from closed mindedness; let us
Be large in thought, in word, in deed.
Let us be done with faultfinding, and
Leave off self-seeking.
May we put away all pretense and
Meet each other face-to-face, without
Self-pity and without prejudice.
May we never be hasty in our judgment
And be always generous and helpful.
Teach us to put into action our better
Impulses, straightforward and unafraid.
Let us take time for the right things. Make us
Grow calm, serene, and gentle.
Grant that we may realize it is the
Little things that create difference,
That in the big things in life we are one.
And may we strive to touch and know
The great common heart of us all;
And O God, let us not forget to be kind.

Living the Way We Pray

I knelt to pray when day was done
And prayed: "O Lord, bless everyone,
And lift from each heart the pain,
And let the sick be well again."

And then the next day when I did awake,
I carelessly went on my way.
The whole day long I did not try
To wipe a tear from any eye.

I did not try to share the load
Of any brother on the road.
I did not even go to see
The sick man just next door to me.

Yet once again when day was done
I prayed: "O Lord, bless everyone."
But as I prayed, to my ear
There came a voice that whispered clear:

"Pause, hypocrite, before you pray:
Whom have you tried to bless today?
God's sweetest blessings always go
By hands that serve Him here below."

I Will Do the Footwork

Creator, my spiritual and emotional growth and the
    fulfillment of the Twelve Step promises are not
    solely gifts I receive without any effort on my part.
I must earn the results by serious, dedicated work.
I pray to use the Steps as tools to do the work.
I will keep my mind open.
I will develop an attitude of rigorous honesty.
I will rid myself of denial and deceit.
I will let go of old ideas.
I will ask for help from my fellow members.
I will work on my shortcomings.
I will continue to make amends.
I will not be satisfied with half-measures.
I will follow spiritual instructions.
God, You give me directions clearly.
I will do the footwork; this I pray.

Karen C.'s Prayer

Today, I pray, I will:

Talk to someone who can help me;
Own my true destiny;
Compliment someone;
Get to know myself better;
Work to create a promising future;
Take advantage of my opportunities;
Allow myself to feel whole;
Use my support system;
Be honorable in my intentions;
Be inspired by the achievements of others;
Have the courage to own the truth;
Act as if there are no obstacles;
Treat myself and others with respect.

Today and from now on I will end
Every prayer with "Thy will be done."

A New Freedom and Happiness

Dear God, I remember the days that were controlled by my desires. The constant need to bow to the demands of my addiction. It made all decisions for me. There was a false freedom and a small bit of happiness. Thank You, God, for helping me work the first nine Steps of our program. I am no longer a slave to my addictions. Freedom has come with abstinence; so has joy, gratitude, and love for others and myself. I have more work to do. God help me on my journey.

Today I Will Trust

Today, I will stop straining to know
What I don't know,
To see what I can't see,
To understand what I don't yet understand.
I will trust that being is sufficient,
And let go of my need to figure things out.

If I'm Discouraged Today

If I'm discouraged today, God of my understanding, let me be able to give thanks for my recovery, my health, my family, and my friends. If I'm discouraged today, let me remember the sadness and problems before recovery. Let me appreciate today and how much better it is than the life I left behind. If I'm discouraged today, may I remember my spiritual journey is the sometimes painful process of learning to let go of things that are not important.

Unrealistic Expectations

Thank You, Father, that I have stopped undermining my happiness with unrealistic expectations. I said I wanted to be happy, but my past actions told a different story. I held on to resentments because I expected life to be fair. I expected to be given all the good things in life simply because I thought I deserved to have them handed to me. Thank You, Father, for helping me get rid of unrealistic expectations. I will make fewer crazy demands on myself, others, and life in general.

Am I Willing?

Dear Higher Power, help me:

To forget what I have done for other people, and to remember what other people have done for me.

To ignore what the world owes me, and to think what I owe the world.

To put my rights in the background, and my duties in the middle distance, and my chances to do a little more than my duty in the foreground.

To see that my fellow members are just as real as I am, and to try to look behind their faces to their hearts, as hungry for joy as mine is.

To own that probably the only good reason for my existence is not what I can get out of life, but what I can give to life.

To close my book of complaints against the management of the universe and look for a place where I can sow a few seeds of happiness—am I willing to do these things even for a day?

Then I have a good chance of staying with the program.

Instinctively Know

God, I pray the instincts that once compelled me toward addiction will continue to be redirected toward solving problems. By working the Steps, I have learned to face up to and solve the problems of everyday living that used to cause me to seek relief in my addiction. I trust I can handle situations with common sense and the help of my friends.

My Worth

I pray to remember that my worth is not determined by my show of outward strength, or the volume of my voice, or the thunder of my accomplishments. It is to be seen, rather, in terms of the nature and depth of my commitments, the genuineness of my friendships, the sincerity of my purpose, the quiet courage of my convictions, my capacity to accept life on life's terms, and my willingness to continue "growing up." This I pray.

I Promise Myself!

Today I pray:

To promise myself to be so strong that nothing can disturb my peace of mind.

To talk health, happiness, and prosperity to every person I meet.

To make all of my friends feel that there is something in them.

To look at the sunny side of everything and make my optimism come true.

To think only of the best, to work only for the best, and to expect only the best.

To be just as enthusiastic about the success of others as I am about my own.

To forget the mistakes of the past and press on to the greater achievements of the future.

To wear a cheerful countenance at all times and give every living creature I meet a smile.

To give so much time to the improvement of myself that I have no time to criticize others.

To be too large for worry, too noble for anger, too strong for fear, and too happy to permit the presence of trouble.

Possibilities Prayer

I know, dear God, that my part in this program is going to be a thrilling and endless adventure. Despite all that has happened to me already, I know that I have just begun to grow. I have just begun to open to Your love. I have just begun to touch the varied lives You are using me to change. I have just begun to sense the possibilities ahead. And these possibilities, I am convinced, will continue to unfold into ever new and richer adventures, not only for the rest of my reborn days but also through eternity.

STEP ELEVEN

❖

Attunement and Spirituality

A PROMISE TO LISTEN

·

OUR SAVIOR

·

OUR TRUTH AND JOY

·

OUR MENTOR

·

OUR WORLD

Our Higher Power is many things:
A Teacher, a Shield, a Shelter.
If we don't listen, though,
We will hear nothing.

Eleventh Step Prayer

Higher Power, as I understand You, I pray to keep open my connection with You and to keep it clear from the confusion of daily life. Through my prayers and meditations I ask especially for freedom from self-will, rationalization, and wishful thinking. I pray for the guidance of correct thought and positive action. Your will, Higher Power, not mine, be done.

For the Spirit of Prayer

Help me, Higher Power, to cultivate the habit of prayer. Enable me to know Your will. I pray I may conform my actions to the demands of Your will. I will pray with concentration of my mind, and I will pray with all my soul. I will pray to You in words of devotion with all my heart. I will pray to You aloud, and I will pray to You in silence. For You hear my prayers, even in thought, and measure my feelings and know my aspirations. I will pray, O God, that prayer may lift me to You and make me Yours.

Eleventh Step Meeting Opening Prayer

We come together to fulfill a call to community and to
nurture one another into Being.

To practice engaging in God within ourselves and one
another.

To share the way we live, love, struggle, and dare to be,
that this community will be inspiring to ourselves
and others.

We pray to vigilantly seek within ourselves a God
Presence that enables us to embrace our humanity
and to step into the Spiritual Experience of mind-
fully living fully, loving excessively, and entering
courageously into the depths of Being.

We pray to be more adequately God-bearers—a source
of life, love, and Being to others.

To be changed, opened, sensitized, and compassionate.

To witness to one another the profound ways that
prayer and meditation have changed us.

To share the healing Power of God, which is Love.

We give thanks for our personal relationship with God.

The Peace of Meditation

So we may know God better
And feel His quiet power,
Let us daily keep in silence
A meditation hour.
For to understand God's greatness
And to use His gifts each day,
The soul must learn to meet Him
In a meditative way.
For our Father tells His children
That if they would know His will.
They must seek Him in the silence
When all is calm and still.

For nature's greatest forces
Are found in quiet things,
Like softly falling snowflakes
Drifting down on angels' wings,
Or petals dropping soundlessly
From a lovely full-blown rose.
God comes closest to us
When our souls are in repose.
So let us plan with prayerful care
To always allocate
A certain portion of each day
To be still and meditate.

Paul D.'s Prayer

We thank You, dear Lord, for giving us Bill and Dr. Bob and for Your divine guidance and direction in their creation of our fellowship and program.

We thank You, dear Lord, for Your blessings and protection of our fellowship and our program in past decades, and we pray, dear Lord, that You will continue to bless and protect our fellowship and our program of Alcoholics Anonymous, always. We thank You, dear Lord, for the countless number of alcoholics for whom You have lifted the bonds of alcohol and allowed us to get sober, live sober lives, and die sober deaths.

We pray, dear Lord, that You will hear the prayers and the cries for help from the still sick and suffering alcoholics and send them to us.

We pray, dear Lord, that we remain forever humble and grateful and always worthy to receive and keep this precious gift of sobriety that You have bestowed upon us, and for all the benefits, gifts, and many, many blessings that we have received from the program of Alcoholics Anonymous, we thank You, dear Lord.

Darkness to Light

Lord, I believe that You will reward each person according to his or her good works. Thank You for turning my darkness into light and for comforting me during my trials and low spots so that I may comfort and encourage others. Set Your word always before me so that I might remember Your great and awesome deeds. You are a faithful and just Teacher.

Sobriety Prayer

If I speak in the tongues of men and even of angels, but have not sobriety, I am a noisy gong or a clanging cymbal. And if I have prophetic powers and understand all mysteries and all knowledge, and if I have all faith, so as to move mountains, but have not sobriety, I am nothing. If I give away all that I have, and if I deliver my body to be burned, but have not sobriety, I gain nothing.

When I am sober, I am patient and kind. When I am sober, I am not jealous nor boastful, nor arrogant or rude. When I am sober, I do not insist on my own way. When I am sober, I am not irritable or resentful. I do not rejoice at wrong as I used to do but rejoice in what is right.

When I am sober, I can bear all things, believe in all things, hope all things, and endure all things.

Sobriety never ends and never fails.

When I was using, I spoke like an arrogant child, thought like a stubborn child, and reasoned like a rebellious child. When I chose sobriety for my life, I gave up my childish ways.

So faith, hope, love, and sobriety abide, but for me, the most important has to be sobriety, for without it, I cannot have the other three, nor can I ever have the serenity I yearn to possess.

Against Temptations

May the strength of my Higher Power guide me.
May the power of God preserve me.
May the wisdom of my Higher Power instruct me.
May the hand of God protect me.
May the way of my Higher Power direct me.
May His shield defend me.
And may the presence of, and belief in,
    my Higher Power guard me against
    the temptations of the world.

Jumping-Off Place

O Lord, remind me of when I could not imagine life either with alcohol or without it. I knew loneliness such as few know. I was at the jumping-off place.

I wished for the end.

The program, the fellowship, and my surrender to You have shown me how to get out from under. This new way of living has not consigned me to a life that is stupid, boring, and glum.

I have found a release from care, boredom, and worry. Life means something at last. My imagination has been fired. I believe the most satisfactory years of my existence lie ahead. Thank You, God.

Seeking Serenity

Higher Power, when I was using, I chased an elusive thing called serenity. My journeys outside reality brought a false peace. When I returned to reality, I found harshness and pain, which caused me to run back to using. Run, escape, pain; run, escape, pain.

Then something happened. My addiction wouldn't let me escape anymore. All that was left was the pain.

Recovery has shown me reality, not the problem. Trying to escape reality is the problem. Finding You and the Twelve Steps and turning my life and will over to You have created a reality of inner peace and strength. I pray and believe and trust these changes in recovery are necessary and good for me.

God Is Enough

Lord, I am grateful that when I got to the bottom and there was nothing left but You, I found that You were enough. My surrender and growing spirituality grant me serenity when surrounded with turmoil. I have an active concern for the well-being of other people. My spiritual growth has helped me, through my attitudes and actions, to better live with myself, You, and others.

When Agitated or Doubtful

Dear God, as I go through my day I pause, when agitated or doubtful, and ask You for the right thought or action. I need to constantly remind myself that I am no longer running the show and humbly say to myself many times each day, "Thy will be done."

The Gifts I Ask

These are the gifts I ask of Thee,
Spirit Serene:
Strength for the daily task,
Courage to face the road,
Good cheer to help me
Bear the traveler's load;
And for the hours that come between,
An inward joy in all things heard and seen.

The Universal Prayer

Eternal Reality,
You are everywhere.
You are infinite unity, truth, and love;
You permeate our souls,
Every corner of the universe, and beyond.

To some of us, You are father, friend, or partner.
To others, Higher Power, Higher Self, or Inner Self.
To many of us, You are all these and more.
You are within us and we are within You.

We know You forgive our trespasses
If we forgive ourselves and others.
We know You protect us from destructive temptation
If we continue to seek Your help and guidance.
We know You provide us food and shelter today
If we but place our trust in You and try to do our best.
Give us this day knowledge of Your will for us
    and the power to carry it out.
For Yours is infinite power and love,
Forever.

I Will

Higher Power,
I will tell You the truth until I can tell others,
I will trust in You until I can trust in others,
I will pray for Your will and not my own,
I will not turn away from the addict who still suffers,
I will pray for mercy and not praise,
I will pray for humility and not righteousness,
I will continue to turn my life over to You
    so I may be restored to greater sanity.

Fellow Travelers

Higher Power, who fills our whole life, and whose presence we find wherever we go, preserve us who travel the road of recovery, surround us with Your loving care, protect us from every danger, and bring us safely to our journey's end.

Direct and Guide My Journey

O Lord, direct and guide my steps on my journey,
    and let me travel in health, joy, and peace.
Keep me from traps and dangers, and protect me
    from any enemies I might meet along the way.
Bless and protect my journey!
Let me win favor in Your eyes and in the sight of those
    around me.
Blessed are You, O Lord,
    Who hears and grants our prayers.

God's Love

I pray that I may walk in Your love, God. I pray that as I go, I may feel the spring of Your power in my steps and the joy of Your love in my heart. A consciousness of Your loving presence makes all life different. You have brought me relief from the cares and worries of my daily life. I pray for the freedom and serenity of a sober life.

The Joy of Right Living

With bended knees, with hands outstretched,
I hope for the effective expression
Of Your Spirit working within me:
For this love and understanding, truth and justice;
For wisdom to know the false from the real
That I might lessen the sufferings of my fellows.
You are love, understanding, wisdom, and virtue.
Let us love one another,
Let us practice mercy and forgiveness,
Let us have peace, born of fellowship.
Let my joy be of right living, of doing good to others.
Happiness is for us whose happiness flows to others.

Prayer of St. Francis of Assisi

Lord, make me an instrument of Your peace!
Where there is hatred, let me sow love.
Where there is injury, pardon.
Where there is doubt, faith.
Where there is despair, hope.
Where there is darkness, light.
Where there is sadness, joy.

O Divine Master, grant that I may not so much seek
To be consoled as to console.
To be understood as to understand.
To be loved as to love.
For it is in giving that we receive.
It is in pardoning that we are pardoned.
It is in dying that we are born to eternal life.

Countless Gifts of Love

Now thank we all our God,
With heart and hands and voices,
Who wondrous things has done,
In whom His world rejoices;
Who from our mother's arms
Has blessed us on our way
With countless gifts of love
And still is ours today.

O may this bounteous God,
Through all our life be near us,
With ever joyful hearts
And blessed peace to cheer us,
And keep us in His grace,
And guide us when perplexed,
And free us from all ills
In this world and the next.

Count Your Blessings

Count your many blessings, name them one by one;
Count your many blessings, see what God has done!

Your Gift

Thank You, Higher Power, for Your gift of recovery, that through this program I have come to know myself better than ever before, and that I have come to know others better as well. I pray that I may be eternally grateful for this, Your blessing.

Prayer to Know

Grant it to me, Higher Power:
To know that which is worth knowing,
To love that which is worth loving,
To praise that which pleases You most,
To work for that which helps others.

Grant it to me:
To distinguish with true judgment things that differ,
    and above all to search out, and to do what is most
    pleasing to You.

The Weight of the World

O God of many names, bless You for lifting the weight of the world off my shoulders. It was never mine to carry in the first place. Surrendering my will to You has removed the loneliness and isolation that addiction placed within me. I need other people. I need their help. The key to unlocking the many gifts of recovery is asking for help. Your direction and love have taught me to ask for help and to help when I am asked.

Reliance on God

O Higher Power,
Never let me think
that I can stand by myself,
and not need You.

We Are Students

Dear God, once again, we are students.
In recovery we are learning the secrets of living completely.
In recovery we have cleared our thinking of obsessions, dependencies, denials, fears, resentments, and other destructive habits that have ruled us.
Dear God, through Your wisdom we have opened our minds to accept and our hearts to understand.

Dear God, in my troubled years I remembered my school days as perhaps the happiest of my life.
I thought they were gone.
But I've found them again through You, the program, and my many teachers.
I love being back in school.
Thank You, God.

Cleveland AA Prayer, 1941

God, You have been our dwelling place in all
generations
Before the mountains were brought forth, or even the
earth and the world were made.
We thank You for having brought us safely to this day
of our lives and
Having taught us to live one day at a time in Your
work.
We pray that You will guide our footsteps tomorrow,
help us as we help ourselves, and help us as we help
others to do Your will.
And we pray that You will extend your special mercy
to those afflicted, as we have been, but who have
not yet been brought from darkness to light.

Lead Me and Guide Me

Almighty God, I humbly pray,
Lead me and guide me through this day.
Cast out my selfishness and sin,
Open my heart to let You in.
Help me now as I blindly stray
Over the pitfalls along the way.
Let me have courage to face each task,
Invest me with patience and love, I ask.
Care for me through each hour today,
Strengthen and guard me now, I pray.

As I forgive, forgive me too,
Needing Your mercy as I do.
Oh, give me Your loving care,
Never abandon me to despair.
Yesterday's wrongs I would seek to right,
Make me more perfect in Your sight.
Oh, teach me to live as best I can,
Use me to help my fellowman.
Save me from acts of bitter shame,
    I humbly ask it in Your name.

Wisdom

Father of Light, You have promised
To give wisdom generously
To all who ask in faith.
Please give me wisdom;
Make me wise to know Your way for me,
Wise to make good decisions,
Wise to be useful to others,
And wise to understand Your word.
May Your Spirit give me wisdom
That I may know Your will,
That I may honor You
And find pleasure in obeying You.

Language of the Heart

Dear God, You know my needs before I ask, my heart before I pray, and my gratitude before I even offer my thanks. You understand me better than I understand myself, and I thank You for communicating with me in the language of the heart.

Wealth, Power, Fame

Dear God, I pray to remember
I will not care overly much for
Wealth, or power, or fame,
Or one day I will meet someone
Who cares for none of these things,
And then I will realize
How poor I have become.

Serenity and Peace

As I have entered the Realm of Spirit,
   after shaking the bondage of addiction
   through the love, encouragement, deep concern,
   and help from newfound friends,
   I've begun to know what serenity feels like.
Peace of mind is new to me.
Serenity becomes refreshing and comfortable
   as I realize I am free and able to make
   sound choices for my life.
That climate encourages serenity and peace.
God, help me to grow toward maturity, serenity,
   and peace of mind.

Prayer for Protection

The light of God surrounds me;
The love of God enfolds me;
The power of God protects me;
The presence of God watches over me;
Wherever I am, God is!

Happiness Prayer from West Africa

I am happy because You have accepted me, dear God.
Sometimes I do not know what to do with all my
     happiness.
I swim in Your grace like a whale in the ocean.
The saying goes "The ocean never dries up," but we
     know Your love also never fails.
Dear Lord, Your love is my happiness.

To Go Outdoors Each Day

Grant me, O Lord, the ability to be alone.
May it be my custom to go outdoors each day
Among the trees and grasses,
Among all growing things.
And there may I be alone,
And enter into prayer
To talk with You,
The One I belong to.

A Summer Prayer

Long warm days . . .
The pace of life slows . . .
A time of picnics, and rest in the shade . . .
A time to celebrate the Spirit of Nature.

Father of Light,
    help me rest awhile in the cooling shade
    of Your presence.
Slow down my restless heart and anxious mind
    and fill me with gentle compassion for all
    Your people.
As the program teaches me, this I pray, to
    "fit ourselves to be of maximum service to God
    and the people about us."

A Fitting Tribute

If my lips could sing as many songs
    as there are waves in the sea;
If my tongue could sing as many hymns
    as the ocean billows;
If my mouth filled the whole sky with praise;
If my face shone like the sun;
If my hands were to soar in the sky
    like powerful eagles
And my feet run across mountains
    like a powerful deer;
All that would be not enough
To pay fitting tribute
To You, O Lord my God.

Thanking You for Little Things

I thank You for the house in which I live,
For the gray roof on which the raindrops slant;
I thank You for a garden and the slim young shoots
That mark the old-fashioned things I plant.

I thank You for a daily task to do,
For books that are my ships with golden wings.
For mighty gifts let others offer praise—
Lord, I thank You for little things.

Be at Peace

Do not look forward in fear to the changes of life,
    rather look to them with full hope that as
    they arise, God will lead you safely through
        all things.
    And when you cannot stand it,
    God will carry you in His arms.
Do not fear what will happen tomorrow.
    The same God who cares for you
    today will take care of you today and every day.
    God will either shield you from suffering
    or will give you unfailing strength to bear it.
Be patient and put aside all anxious thoughts and
    imaginations.

Amazing Grace

Amazing grace! How sweet the sound
That saved a wretch like me.
I once was lost, but now am found,
Was blind, but now I see.

'Twas grace that taught my heart to fear,
And grace my fears relieved.
How precious did that grace appear
The hour I first believed.

Through many dangers, toils, and snares,
I have already come.
'Tis grace has brought me safe thus far,
And grace will lead me home.

When we've been here ten thousand years,
Bright shining as the sun,
We've no less days to sing God's praise
Than when we'd first begun.

STEP TWELVE

✻

Service and Usefulness

WHAT WE LEARNED

·

NEWFOUND COMMUNITY

·

FOREVERMORE

In the spiritual world,
Everything we may receive
Comes from giving.

Twelfth Step Prayer

Dear God,

My spiritual awakening continues to unfold. The help I have received I shall pass on and give to others, both in and out of the fellowship. For this opportunity I am grateful.

I pray most humbly to continue walking day by day on the road of spiritual progress. I pray for the inner strength and wisdom to practice the principles of this way of life in all I do and say. I need You, my friends, and the program every hour of every day. This is a better way to live.

The Twelve Steps Prayer

Power greater than myself, as I understand You, I willingly admit that without Your help I am powerless over alcohol, and my life has become unmanageable. I believe You can restore me to sanity. I turn my life and my will over to You. I have made a searching and fearless moral inventory of myself, and I admit to You, to myself, and to another the exact nature of my wrongs. I am entirely ready to have You remove these defects of character. I humbly ask You to remove my shortcomings. I have made direct amends to all persons I have harmed, except when to do so would injure them or others. I will continue to take personal inventory, and when I am wrong, I will promptly admit it. I seek through prayer and meditation to improve my conscious contact with You and pray only for knowledge of Your will for me and the power to carry it out.

Grant me the grace to carry the message of Your help unto others and to practice the principles of the Twelve Steps in all my affairs.

I Try to Help People

I try to help people experience their spiritual connectedness by helping them get in touch with both their tenderness and their power. I don't think there's such a thing as instant intimacy or instant spirituality—they are things that evolve in us. To reach them, we need to see that we are born to evolve. It is a growing thing—and there is no fear in it. Not that we haven't heard the message before. It's what Christ talked about, and the Buddha, and others. But in the past, most of us said, "They're beyond us, they're divine . . . we're nothing but humans, so we can't make the same connection." But now, we're beginning to know we can.

The Four Absolutes

Absolute Honesty
Both with ourselves and with others, in word, deed, and thought.

Absolute Unselfishness
To be willing, wherever possible, to help others who need our help.

Absolute Love
You shall love the Lord with all your heart, and with all your soul, and with all your mind. And . . . you shall love your neighbor as yourself.

Absolute Purity
Purity of mind, of body, and of purpose.

Benefiting Others

Dear God, bless You for bringing me from the lowest depths of existence. What excitement has come to me when I discovered I am not a worthless human being. When I drank and used, I thought I was doomed to be incompetent, unworthy, and a dishonest person. No more. My escape from the depths of despair has made me feel needed and trusted. Others listen to my story of how I was, what happened, and what I am like today. Lord, bless You for making me a helpful person by sharing those very experiences that made me feel worthless.

Part of the Solution

Dear Lord, remind me that when I was practicing my addiction, I traveled alone.

No relationship was more important. I was a hostage in a prison of chemicals. The fellowship and Your guidance have broken that grip of isolation. I pray to remain grateful to the men and women who share their experience, strength, and hope. The fellowship is a circle of spiritual vitality that energizes me when I'm willing to join hands. Alone I am the problem. Together with others, I am part of the solution.

God of Our Life

God of our Life,
There are days when the burdens we carry
Hurt our shoulders and weigh us down,
When our lives have no music in them
And our hearts are lonely.
Flood our path with light, we pray.
Turn our eyes to where the skies are full of promise;
Tune our hearts to brave music;
Give us a sense of fellowship with others,
And lift our spirits so we may encourage
Others who journey with us on the road of recovery.

Uselessness and Self-Pity

Dear Lord, when I was deep within the bewilderment and agony of my addiction, I often moaned, "What's the use? Nobody cares." I was a lost person. I thought I was incapable of doing anything worthwhile for anyone, including myself. Shame and guilt made me wallow in self-pity. By working the program and focusing on positive things, I have changed. I have become more useful to myself and others. By recognizing my limitations and avoiding perfectionism, I've moved away from self-pity toward self-worth.

Do the Right Thing

Help me, Higher Power, to get out of myself, to stop always thinking of what I need. Show me the way I can be helpful to others and supply me with the strength to do the right thing.

The 23rd-1/2 Psalm

The Lord is my sponsor! I shall not want.

He directs me to go to many meetings.

He desires me to sit back, relax, and listen with an open mind.

He restores my soul, my sanity, and my health.

He leads me in the paths of sobriety, serenity, and fellowship for my own sake.

He teaches me to think, to take it easy, to live and let live, and to do first things first.

He teaches me to accept the things I cannot change, teaches me to change the things that I can, and gives me the wisdom to know the difference.

Yea, though I walk through the valley of despair, frustration, guilt, and remorse, I will fear no evil, for God is with me. The program, God's way of life, the Twelve Steps—they comfort me.

Surely sobriety and serenity shall follow me every day of my life, twenty-four hours at a time, as I surrender my will to God and carry the message to others, and I will dwell in the house of my Higher Power, as I understand Him, daily.

Kindness and Service

O Lord, help me always to remember thankfully the work of those who helped me when I needed help. Reward them for their kindness and service, and grant that I may have the will, the time, and the opportunity to do the same for others.

The Fellowship Prayer

Dear Higher Power, I am grateful that:

I am part of the fellowship, one among many, but I am one.

I need to work the Steps for the development of the buried life within me.

Our program may be human in its organization, but it is Divine in its purpose. The purpose is to continue my spiritual awakening.

Participating in the privileges of the movement, I shall share in the responsibilities, taking it upon myself to carry my fair share of the load, not grudgingly, but joyfully.

To the extent that I fail in my responsibilities, the program fails. To the extent that I succeed, the program succeeds.

I shall not wait to be drafted for service to my fellow members. I shall volunteer.

I shall be loyal in my attendance, generous in my giving, kind in my criticism, creative in my suggestions, loving in my attitudes.

I shall give to the program my interest, my enthusiasm, my devotion, and most of all, myself.

My Design

God, my purpose is to help others.
Give me this work,
Till my life shall end
And life
Till my work is done.

Carry This Message

Dear God, I now fully realize how much the program, You, and other people have helped me. It is my responsibility to carry this message to those who still suffer, whether they are in need of our fellowship or are in our fellowship and are struggling today. You have demonstrated to me that life is no longer a dead end without hope. With this gift, I am now able to help others. My spiritual progress is measured by my positive actions. God, You have only asked me to be helpful and to leave the results to You.

Share Strength

Today I will stand up for those who are weak and
   beaten down, for those who are poor and treated
   unfairly, and
I will speak out for those who have no voice and no
   home.
I shall do this to remind myself that I was once one of
   them and could yet become one of them.
In doing this, I save another and keep myself from my
   addiction, my weakness.
This I pray.

When Seeking God

If a person would find God, let that person humbly ask for a chance to believe, and meanwhile let him or her go personally, not by delegate, to a less fortunate brother or sister, helping him or her in need of body and soul.

When a person seeks God, he or she will presently find what is sought. For when a person can leave himself or herself and enter the lives of others, that person leaves his or her own heart open so that God may enter and dwell within.

Our Meeting Room Door

Dear God,
Make the door of this meeting wide enough
To receive all who need love and fellowship
And narrow enough to shut out
All envy, pride, and hate.
Make its threshold smooth enough
To be no stumbling block to anyone,
Nor to those who have strayed,
But rugged enough to turn back
The tempter's power:
Make it a gateway
To Thine eternal kingdom.

The Miracle of Meetings

Thank You, God, for one of the great miracles of Twelve Step recovery—the wisdom, insight, and encouragement I receive in our meetings. As I listen to others share their adventures in letting go, surrendering to Your will, taking inventory, and practicing recovery principles, I always hear something that comforts or challenges me. Often the meetings alert me to a problem I am having and then give me hope and determination to keep pressing on. God, make me ever aware that what I do between meetings is what is really important.

Wesley P.'s Prayer

Dear God, please fill me
With Your loving spirit, and
Let it flow through me
Into the lives of others.
Amen.

I Cannot Pray

I cannot pray the Lord's Prayer and even once say "I."
I cannot pray the Lord's Prayer and even once say "my."
Nor can I pray the Lord's Prayer and not pray for
    another,
And when I ask for daily bread, I must include
    all others.
For others are included in each and every plea,
From the beginning to the end of it, it does not once
    say "me."

My Prayer for You

I thought of you so much today
I went to God in prayer,
To ask Him to watch over you
And show you that we care.

My prayer for you was not for rewards
That you could touch or feel,
But true rewards for happiness
That are so very real.

Like love and understanding
In all the things you do,
And guidance when you need it most
To see your troubles through.

I asked Him for good health for you
So your future could be bright,
And faith to accept life's challenges
And the courage to do what's right.

I gave thanks to Him for granting my prayer
To bring you peace and love.
May you feel the warmth in your life
With God's blessings from above.

For My Sponsee

Dear God, You have placed a new sponsee for me to welcome to our recovery world. I pray that this person will be filled with joy, peace, and serenity if it is Your will. I'll try to help. I'm not a professional counselor, medical consultant, or financial expert. I hope to be this individual's friend. I have only my experience, strength, and hope to share. I will teach the ways of the program and help this person find his or her own answers. I can't prevent a relapse but can only carry this message—and help my sponsee find his or her own spirituality. I will listen and hear and learn from this person. I will love this individual until he or she can experience self-love—and beyond. Thank You, God, for this opportunity.

For Those Who Have Relapsed

O God of all mercies and comfort, Who helps us in time of need, we humbly ask You to behold, visit, and relieve those who have relapsed for whom our prayers are desired. Look upon them with the eyes of Your mercy; comfort them with a sense of Your goodness; preserve them from the temptations of their addiction; and give them patience under their affliction. In Your time, restore them to the program and physical, mental, and spiritual health. And help them, we pray, to listen, believe, and do Your will.

The Victims of Addiction

O blessed Lord, You ministered to all who came to You.

Look with compassion upon all who through addiction have lost their health and freedom. Restore to them the assurance of Your unfailing mercy; remove from them the fears that beset them; strengthen them in the work of their recovery; and to those who care for them, give patient understanding and persevering love.

For Families Torn by Addiction

We pray, O God of hope,
For all families
Whose lives are torn and disrupted
By addiction.
Enable them to identify the illness.
Strengthen them to seek help.
Bless them with the power of Your love,
Which imparts transformation and wholeness
To those who trust in Your name.
Grant that as they walk this tortured road,
They may journey together
And bind close in the bond of love.
Amen.

For Loved Ones Far Away

O Great Spirit, whose care reaches to the farthest parts
    of the earth,
We humbly ask You to see and bless those whom we
    love
Who are now absent from us,
And defend and protect them from all dangers of mind,
    body, and spirit.

Let Go, Let God

Higher Power, help me to understand:

To "let go" does not mean to stop caring; it means I can't do it for someone else.

To "let go" is not to enable but to allow learning from natural consequences.

To "let go" is to admit powerlessness, which means the outcome is not in my hands.

To "let go" is not to try to change or blame another; it's to make the most of myself.

To "let go" is not to care for but to care about.

To "let go" is not to fix but to be supportive.

To "let go" is not to judge but to allow another to be a human being.

To "let go" is not to protect; it's to permit another to face reality.

To "let go" is not to deny but to accept.

To "let go" is not to nag, scold, or argue but instead to search out my own shortcomings and correct them.

To "let go" is not to adjust everything to my desires but to take each day as it comes and cherish myself in it.

Thank You for My Friends

I give You thanks, O God, for those who mean so much to me. For those friends in the program I can go to anytime. For those with whom I can talk and keep nothing back, knowing that they will not laugh at my defects or dreams. For those whose fellowship makes it easier to be good. For those who, by their warning, have held me back from making mistakes I might have made. Above all, I thank You, God, for giving me all of my recovery friends, who are bound to me by a common problem; together we find a common solution.

I Am Thankful For . . .

God, I am thankful for the people to whom I can relate
    in all situations.
I am grateful for all of them—
For those called "family" who provide community,
For those called "sponsors" who give guidance,
For those called "enemies" who help me see my faults,
For those called "colleagues" who share responsibility,
For those called "teachers" who instruct me,
For those called "helpers" who enable me to seek help,
For those called "comforters" who dry my tears,
    unafraid of my weeping.

Things to Give

Today, I pray I may give:

To my enemy:	Forgiveness.
To my opponent:	Tolerance.
To my customer:	Service.
To a friend:	Kindness.
To all people:	Charity.
To my family:	My heart.
To every child:	A good example.
To myself:	Respect.
To You, Higher Power:	LOVE
	With all my heart,
	With all my soul,
	With all my mind.

The Twelve Rewards

Spirit of the Universe,
I humbly ask for Your help so I may continue to realize
the rewards of recovery:

Hope instead of desperation.
Faith instead of despair.
Courage instead of fear.
Peace of mind instead of confusion.
Self-respect instead of self-contempt.
Self-confidence instead of helplessness.
The respect of others instead of pity and contempt.
A clean conscience instead of a sense of guilt.
Real friendship instead of loneliness.
A clean pattern of life instead of a purposeless existence.
The love and understanding of my family instead of
their doubts and fears.
The freedom of a happy life instead of the bondage
of addiction.

Peace and Justice for All

Spirit of the Universe,
Lead us from death to life,
From falsehood to truth.
Lead us from despair to hope,
From fear to trust.
Let peace fill our hearts,
Our world, our universe.
Let us dream together,
Pray together,
Work together,
To build one world
Of peace and justice for all.

High Flight

Oh, I have slipped the surly bonds of earth
And danced the skies on laughter-silvered wings,
Sunward I've climbed and joined the tumbling mirth
Of sun-split clouds—and done a hundred things
You have not dreamed of—wheeled and soared
    and swung
High in the sunlit silence. Hov'ring there
I've chased the shouting wind along and flung
My eager craft through footless halls of air.
Up, up the long, delirious, burning blue
I've topped the windswept heights with easy grace
Where never lark nor even eagle flew.
And while with silent, lifting mind I've trod
The high untrespassed sanctity of space,
Put out my hand, and touched the face of God.

NIGHTFALL

❅

Prayers to End Your Day with Serenity

QUIETUDE

Night will fall quietly if you let it.

At Night

Day is done;
Gone the sun
From the lake, from the hills, from the sky.
May I safely rest,
For all is well!
God is near.

Sleep Mantra

Repeat this mantra or chant as necessary:

Ang Sang Wahe Guru
(pronounced "ahng sahng whah-hay gu-roo")

Meaning: The Infinite Being, God, is with me,
and vibrates in every molecule and cell of my being.

The Morning Light

Lord of the night,
Be with me through the hours of darkness.
Let all my questions,
Problems, decisions,
Be enveloped in sleep
That through the mystery
Of the sleeping mind
The difficulties of this day
Will be seen to be easier
In the morning light.
Into Your hands, O Lord,
I commit my spirit.

Rest

Go with each of us to rest;
If we awake, temper to them the dark hours
    of watching;
And when the day returns, return to us,
Our Sun and Comforter, and call us up with
Morning faces and with morning hearts
Eager to labor, eager to be happy
If happiness would be our portion,
And if the day be marked for sorrow,
We are strong to endure it.

Deep Peace

May God shield you.
May God bring you
    to the land of deep peace.
Deep peace of the running wave to you,
Deep peace of the flowing air to you,
Deep peace of the quiet earth to you,
Deep peace of the shining stars to you,
Deep peace of the gentle night to you.
Moon and stars pour their healing light on you.
Deep peace of God, the Light of the World,
Deep peace of God.

Live a Little, Just to Please

Can you say today in honesty
As the hours slip by so fast,
That you've helped a single person
Of the many you have passed?

Did you waste the day, or lose it?
Was it well or properly spent?
Did you leave a trail of kindness
Or mementos of discontent?

Have you given God a moment
In humble, devout prayer?
Have you talked with Him in honesty
To let Him know you care?

As you close your eyes in slumber,
Do you think that God would say,
"You have made the world much better,
For you *lived a lot* today?"

Prayer for the Hurried

Lord, slow me down.

Ease the pounding of my heart by quieting my mind. Steady my hurried pace. Give me, in the confusion of my day, the calmness of the everlasting hills. Break the tension of my nerves and muscles. Help me to know the magical, restoring power of sleep.

Teach me to take minute vacations by slowing down to look at a flower or a cloud, to chat with a friend, to pat a dog, to read a few lines from a good book. Remind me that the race is not always to the swift; that there is more to life than increasing speed.

Let me look upward into the branches of the towering oak and know that it grew great and strong because it grew slowly and well.

Lord, slow me down. Inspire me to send my roots deep into the soil of life's enduring values that I may grow toward the stars of my great destiny.

Someone Does Care

I found God in the morning; we just sat and talked.
I kept Him near me, everywhere I walked.
I called on God at noontime, a heart filled
    with despair.
I felt His quiet presence; I knew He was there.
We met again at sunset, the waning of the day.
I had made Him happy; I had lived His way.
Then when at bedtime I knelt silently in prayer,
Again His gentle presence I felt. Someone does care.

Thank You for Today

Good night, Lord.

Thank You for today, for my sanity, for my life, for the people surrounding me, for fellowship and my recovery.

Tonight, I also pray for the addicts who still suffer. I pray that You relieve their suffering if only for a moment, a moment that may bring them closer to You and recovery.

I look forward to tomorrow and another day of sobriety.

List of Readings and Attributions

Opening Prayer

Daybreak: Prayers to Start Your Day
with Intentionality and Mindfulness

Step One: Honesty and Beginnings

Step Two: Hope and Belief

Step Three: Faith and Commitment

Step Four: Courage and Truth

Step Five: Integrity and Trust

Step Six: Willingness

Step Seven: Humility and Surrender

Step Eight: Reflection and Responsibility

Step Nine: Love and Restitution

Step Ten: Growth and Vigilance

Step Eleven: Atonement and Spirituality

Step Twelve: Service and Usefulness

Other Titles That May Interest You

Easy Does It
A Book of Daily 12 Step Meditations
BILL P., co-author of *The 12 Step Prayer Guide*

"Easy does it." To think, a few simple words can change a day, and a few simple days can change a life. We often forget the importance of recovery slogans. They drape the walls of our meetings, they ride the bumpers of cars, and they spring from every sponsor's mouth—for good reason. Sayings and slogans are behavioral guides and reminders.

Easy Does It, written by the authors of *The Twelve Step Prayer Book*, is a Twelve Step recovery book grounded in calming reflection and introspection. It reminds us, with a few simple words each day, to work a recovery full of patience, mindfulness, and spirituality. It's our job to remember.

Order No. 6424; also available as an ebook

A Day at a Time
Daily Reflections for Recovering People
ANONYMOUS

A Day at a Time is based on the spiritual foundation of Twelve Step recovery. These daily reflections and prayers offer inspiration, comfort, and hope to those of us recovering from addictions. *A Day at a Time* also draws upon the wisdom of the world's greatest poets, scholars, and philosophers. This collection of discerning thoughts will provide ample support for each day's newest hurdle.

Order No. 7602; also available as an ebook

For more information about Hazelden publications, please call **800-328-9000** or visit us online at **hazelden.org/bookstore**.

About Hazelden Publishing

As part of the Hazelden Betty Ford Foundation, Hazelden Publishing offers both cutting-edge educational resources and inspirational books. Our print and digital works help guide individuals in treatment and recovery, and their loved ones. Professionals who work to prevent and treat addiction also turn to Hazelden Publishing for evidence-based curricula, digital content solutions, and videos for use in schools, treatment programs, correctional programs, and electronic health records systems. We also offer training for implementation of our curricula.

Through published and digital works, Hazelden Publishing extends the reach of healing and hope to individuals, families, and communities affected by addiction and related issues.

For more information about Hazelden publications, please call **800-328-9000** or visit us online at **hazelden.org/bookstore.**